PRACTICE GRATITUDE:
Find Joy

TJ Sweet

Practice Gratitude: Find Joy

©*2022 by TJ Sweet. All rights reserved. No part of this book may be reproduced or transmitted in any form or by any means, electronic or mechanical, including photocopying, recording, or by any information storage and retrieval system,without permission in writing from the copyright owner.*

Published by Your Online Publicist: February 2022

ISBN: 978-1-63892-162-2 (hc)
ISBN: 978-1-63892-141-7 (sc)

Suite 337 7950 NW, 53rd St.
Miami, Florida 33166 USA
www.youronlinepublicist.com
(800) 419-3014

Printed in United States of America

This book is printed on acid-free paper

FOREWORD

As you read this book, my desire for you is to gain a better understanding of your own ability to control your own thoughts and mindset by reading the messages and practicing the journaling piece. This is impactful and will make a difference in helping you be more present. The messages are different each day so do your best to not let it turn into something heavy or something that makes you lose patience while you internalize each message.

Why Practice Gratitude? Because it forces you to realize you already have the tools to make you happy. We will draw them out together! When you practice gratitude daily, it will make you feel more present and help you realize the abundance of amazing things that you have in your life. Right now. It is easy to get stuck thinking more about the things you wish you had, but gratitude centers you and makes you realize all the great things around you and how lucky you are! My promise to you, your heart and mind will become clearer and allow you to gain a fresh perspective in life.

Instead of that constant sense of lack, gratitude gives a sense of abundance. The biggest shift you will feel will happen when gratitude becomes the center of everything, and it will replace the sense of yearning. I stopped feeling incomplete when I felt grateful for what I had done and for what I had because I finally realized most of my accomplishments or successes came along without me doing anything extraordinary or beyond my everyday potential.

Since you are deciding to Practice Gratitude, my desire is for you to read the message and realize that your troubling thoughts are not uncommon.

Some of the messages will resonate with you in different ways and on different days. This book will meet you where you are and make a positive impact on your heart and mind when the timing is right. With the right mindset, every message will make you think about life with a different perspective.

PRACTICE GRATITUDE: KEEP IT SIMPLE

Practicing Gratitude is simple. Some over complicate it. Focus on thinking about things that you are truly grateful for, don't force the gratitude. To get started, think about things, events, people, abilities and how that would drastically change your life if you lost it or them. For example, the ability to read...should be something we are grateful for, and we should give ourselves credit for working on our reading skills as hard as we did. You shouldn't feel pressure to come up with three different things every day and you must have a thousand different things at the end of the year. It's not about that. Practicing gratitude is a learned skill.

Think through the book and how the sense of feeling grateful feels good. You'll feel lighter and your heart will feel better, and your mind will be much more forward looking. Gratitude can be cultivated if you do this with a spouse, partner, friend, family member, neighbor, work peer, etc. I encourage you to share the messages with others and feel the sense of joy by shining a light of gratitude for another person. Some of the messages will sound like things you have already heard but we are a new person each day. One of the things that excites me about these messages, is even for me, they've hit me at different times throughout my life. I've heard some of them five times in five years and didn't think anything of it, BUT that one time I heard it, it completely changed my life.

Before you get started with Day One...be patient with yourself and the message. I purposely didn't put dates on the pages for you. The most impactful practice of gratitude is a daily practice but start where you are and gain momentum. See this as an opportunity and don't feel an obligation to have been inspired by every message. We are human and that expectation is not realistic.

How to Practice Gratitude

First off, find what works for you. Find a time that works for you on a consistent basis. First thing is to figure out when you are most willing and able to learn or read a message. No right answer here, just when and where works for you. It can be on your lunch break when you have the beginning of your day already in your head and then you're thinking about adding the rest of the day with gratitude. If you are a night person, try it at the end of the day when you are winding down. The message creates thoughts that fill you with peace and calm and help aid sleep. It may also work for you to lie down to get in a good state of mind.

Next, the power behind thinking of two things you appreciate about yourself is because we're typically our biggest critics. We spend more time thinking about losing weight, getting a new job, or being hard on ourselves for a regrettable decision. This section is not just about vanity but rather it's about two things that you've recognized as your gifts, or something you do well or one of the many ways that you add value to other's lives.

For example, it could be your mindset. It could be your patience. It could be your willingness to serve others. There's a lot of great things about you. So, I encourage you to listen to some of those things from people around you or even just think about ways that you feel like you're making a difference in other's lives. It can be as simple or as complex as you want to be. It is not about comparing yourself to other people but it's just recognizing that there are some unique things about you and that we're meant to be different people.

Then comes the daily affirmation "I am" is a moment of pause for your heart and mind. It's easy to get caught up in should'a, could'a, would'a. Having thoughts like, "It's a sunny day and it's a Saturday I should be really happy and productive." You are beating yourself up for not being upbeat and getting your exhaustive list completed. I want you to accept the feeling and move on. "Today, I am feeling anxious." It is okay to allow yourself to be that. Stop beating yourself up. It's counterproductive! When you are happy, writing down that you are truly happy is profound. When you can feel comfortable enough to say that you're happy, it makes a difference in our mind to think I am happy as opposed to being stuck thinking what other people think you should feel all the time. So, it is more of centering yourself and making it ok to not be OK... just don't stay there. When should you do the daily affirmation section? I'm a morning person so it's easier for me in the morning because my brain is running at an optimal level for the first few hours of the day and is open to new thoughts. Repetition is the key to it and the sense of just opening your heart and mind because most of us don't read inspirational messages or even thoughts like that ever. So just commit when you open the book and make a promise to yourself that you are going to do this once a day or do this once a week whatever it is. Sustainability is the goal. Consistency or intensity is really the main thing. So, doing it every day and having it be a chore is not the goal. It's more of letting the book impact you as opposed to having it feel like homework. See this book as an opportunity to change your life, not an obligation.

Last few tips on Gratitude before starting this life-changing journey...

Different areas of your life are going to be more front of mind for you at different times in your life. So if your career is a big focus in your life right now then I encourage you to look at those things about your career that you're grateful for. Maybe if it's a rough time in your relationships or your family or whatever it might be. THE best way out of a challenging time is gratitude. When you let gratitude affect your heart and mind, you will begin to see life for what it is and not what it could have been or should be. #NeverStop believing in your abilities to change the way you think.

Now...take a deep breath, promise yourself that you can, will, and must embrace this journey while you Practice Gratitude and Find Joy. My promise to you is simple...It works if you put in the work.

Surround yourself with people that want to see you flourish. Pay attention to the look in their eyes when you tell them your goals. You can tell they want you to accomplish your goals as much as you do. Stay close to those people because they are special, and they have been divinely sent to be in your life.

I want to dedicate this book to the wonderful people that have filled my heart with joy and gratitude.

I have been inspired by YOU and I appreciate YOU.

Surround yourself with people that want to see you flourish. Pay attention to the look in their eyes when you tell them your goals. You can tell they want you to accomplish your goals as much as you do. Stay close to those people because they are special, and they have been divinely sent to be in your life.

We mirror the people we spend the most time with. Make sure to spend a lot of time with people that encourage, inspire, and support you.

NeverStop.

I am grateful for these three things in my life

1. _____

2. _____

3. _____

I appreciate these two things about myself:

1. _____

2. _____

I am_____.

(POSITIVE AFFIRMATION)

We all have some sort of motivation in our lives. We are either motivated to change or maintain certain aspects of our lives. We just must slow down enough to know why we do what we do. Everything we do affects everything else. Our hearts and minds are always connected. We are either moving towards or away from what we want in life.

Understand what motivates you and surround yourself with more of that. Motivation gets us started but your why keeps you going.

NeverStop.

I am grateful for these three things in my life

1. _____

2. _____

3. _____

I appreciate these two things about myself:

1. _____

2. _____

I am_____.

(POSITIVE AFFIRMATION)

When we truly listen to others, they will tell you a lot more. When someone trusts you to tell you what is on their heart and mind, it is always worth slowing down and being present in the moment. Looking people in the eye and waiting until they are finished speaking shows that you value them.

Always listen to understand, not to reply. We have a lot to learn, and we do not learn while we are talking.

NeverStop.

I am grateful for these three things in my life

1. _____

2. _____

3. _____

I appreciate these two things about myself:

1. _____

2. _____

I am_____.

(POSITIVE AFFIRMATION)

Never lose your sense of wonder and happiness with things that have brought you so much joy for many years. Be amazed and captivated by the beauty that surrounds us and get excited about life. For it is our spirit inside of us that people admire and appreciate. A spirit of love and joy is contagious. Believe in the power of love.

We should always maintain our sense of wonder and take a moment to be quiet and captivated by beauty. Believe in the spirit of life.

NeverStop.

I am grateful for these three things in my life

1. _____

2. _____

3. _____

I appreciate these two things about myself:

1. _____

2. _____

I am_____.
(POSITIVE AFFIRMATION)

No matter what level of success we accomplish, we must always maintain our sense of self and always remember our true value. Do not let success give you an inflated view of what you deserve. Our value is based on who we are, not what we do for a living. Our heart and mind are what makes the difference.

We all have a unique heart and mind that mean a lot to the people around us. No matter what, be humble and know that no one of us is better than all of us.

NeverStop.

I am grateful for these three things in my life

1. _____

2. _____

3. _____

I appreciate these two things about myself:

1. _____

2. _____

I am_____.
(POSITIVE AFFIRMATION)

We must make a difference when we can. Control what we can and let go and trust that everything will work out as it should. Use your energy for good and stay focused on being productive. Don't let stress or anxiety use up your energy. Life is short so use yours for good.

We are all capable of making a difference. When we can, we should. Be the example of what could be and inspire people to believe in people again.

NeverStop.

I am grateful for these three things in my life

1._____

2._____

3._____

I appreciate these two things about myself:

1. _____

2. _____

I am_____.

(POSITIVE AFFIRMATION)

Pay attention in the moment to create memories. Most of what we remember are moments that made us feel something special. Sometimes things happen in a moment, but they last a lifetime. Be present in each moment and use your memories to free your heart and mind.

Minutes, hours, weeks, months, and years go by pretty fast so take time to recognize the moments in your life. Be grateful for each moment you get.

NeverStop.

I am grateful for these three things in my life

1. _____

2. _____

3. _____

I appreciate these two things about myself:

1. _____

2. _____

I am_____.
                    (POSITIVE AFFIRMATION)

Show as much care and compassion as you can. It can be seen, heard, or felt by those around us. Never let day go by without showing compassion for those that are in your life. Always be aware of the state of your heart and mind because it will always lead to your actions. Show people how you think about them by how you treat them and how you act towards them.

We have many ways to communicate our care and compassion for others. Always find a way because it always means a lot.

NeverStop.

I am grateful for these three things in my life

1. _____

2. _____

3. _____

I appreciate these two things about myself:

1. _____

2. _____

I am_____.

(POSITIVE AFFIRMATION)

Be slow to anger and quick to listen. Seek to understand, not judge. We can easily be blinded by fear and anger, but we should always rely on love, joy, and patience to be the light and to help us see life clearly. Rule your own heart, mind, and spirit. Choose love, faith, and hope.

Never allow fear or anger to take place in your heart. If you are full of love and optimism, there will be no more room for anything else.

NeverStop.

I am grateful for these three things in my life

1. _____

2. _____

3. _____

I appreciate these two things about myself:

I am_____.

(POSITIVE AFFIRMATION)

Be encouraged and amazed by the sign of a sunrise. Each day begins with divine beauty, and we must slow down enough to take it in. Sunrises and Sunsets can affect our soul if we let them.

Each day is a day that you have been given to share your heart, mind, and gifts to the world. Never take a sunrise for granted because it was meant just for you to see it.

Always take time to be captivated by sunrises and sunsets. The beauty cannot be described with one word and no photo can truly capture their brilliance. They are meant for our eyes to enjoy and to encourage us.

NeverStop.

I am grateful for these three things in my life

1. _____

2. _____

3. _____

I appreciate these two things about myself:

I am_____.

(POSITIVE AFFIRMATION)

Be compassionate, persistent, joyful, determined, loving and humble. The beauty that you are is exactly what the world needs. Who we are and who we are becoming is going to make a difference in the world. Remain optimistic and shine your light as much as you can, not as much as you were told you should.

Who you are and who you are becoming is a beautiful thing. Be patient and appreciate the journey.

NeverStop.

I am grateful for these three things in my life

1. _____

2. _____

3. _____

I appreciate these two things about myself:

1. _____

2. _____

I am_____.
(POSITIVE AFFIRMATION)

Living a grateful life will stop the regret cycle we can fall in to. Live life appreciating what you have now so you will be at peace knowing that you cherished every moment. We are at our best when we feel the most grateful.

We all have a unique heart and mind that mean a lot to the people around us. No matter what, be humble and know that no one of us is better than all of us.

NeverStop.

I am grateful for these three things in my life

1. _____

2. _____

3. _____

I appreciate these two things about myself:

1. _____

2. _____

I am_____.

(POSITIVE AFFIRMATION)

Be so full of gratitude and thanks that people can see it in your eyes and your smile. Let gratitude affect your heart and your mind. Take time to think about what you are grateful for and share it with others. Slow down enough to truly appreciate the people, things, and opportunities you have in your life.

NeverStop.

I am grateful for these three things in my life

1. _____

2. _____

3. _____

I appreciate these two things about myself:

1. _____

2. _____

I am_____.
(POSITIVE AFFIRMATION)

Nobody knows everything about everything. Continue to learn more about others to help learn more about yourself. Pay attention to lessons learned by others, read books, and ask people about their hindsight so it can be your foresight. We don't always have to learn every lesson ourselves. Be inspired, humble, and optimistic. Great things are coming.

Cultivate the desire to learn and grow. Be humble enough to learn from anyone that you get the opportunity to talk with or see. You can learn from anyone if your heart and mind are open.

NeverStop.

I am grateful for these three things in my life

1. _____

2. _____

3. _____

I appreciate these two things about myself:

1. _____

2. _____

I am_____.

(POSITIVE AFFIRMATION)

Cultivate joy and gratitude each day. As the waves crash into the shore with a peaceful rhythm, we ought to develop a daily rhythm of goodness in our hearts and minds. Celebrate life more often and realize that you have just what you need, and every moment has been prepared just for you. Be optimistic, grateful, and happy... it is a choice we get to make.

Take charge of your state of mind and surround yourself with people that make you grow, want the best for you, and that believe in you. Be grateful for those people every day.

NeverStop.

I am grateful for these three things in my life

1. _____

2. _____

3. _____

I appreciate these two things about myself:

1. _____

2. _____

I am_____.
(POSITIVE AFFIRMATION)

Take time for yourself each day. Write down what is on your mind but just for you to see and reflect on. Holding too much in our minds prevents us from thinking clearly. To be at our best for others, we have to take time to care for ourselves. Love yourself, invest in yourself and believe in yourself.

Never lose your sense of self even when you get busy with life. To be at our best on the outside, we need to take care of our hearts, minds, and bodies.

NeverStop.

I am grateful for these three things in my life

    1. _____

    2. _____

    3. _____

I appreciate these two things about myself:

    1. _____

    2. _____

I am_____.

                    (POSITIVE AFFIRMATION)

If you want to test the nature of something, entrust it to time. Resist the urge to be in a hurry to do everything. We can't see clearly when we rush or fast forward life. Just like we cannot see much in stormy waters, we need to wait until our hearts and minds are more settled. Be patient, have faith, and trust in THE plan.

Since who we become along the way is more important, why rush to the end? If you rush, you may miss the most important part. Put in the work and be patient and trust.

NeverStop.

I am grateful for these three things in my life

1. _____

2. _____

3. _____

I appreciate these two things about myself:

1. _____

2. _____

I am_____.
                              (POSITIVE AFFIRMATION)

There is never a perfect time for you to take action. Don't let the fear of failure stop you from starting that goal, becoming your best, or changing your habits. Never let the odds keep you from doing what you know in your heart you were meant to do. Be led by faith, not fear.

Be encouraged by what you can do and become. We are given the opportunity to fulfill our potential every day. Pay attention to what sets your heart and soul on fire and do more of that.

NeverStop.

I am grateful for these three things in my life

    1. _____

    2. _____

    3. _____

I appreciate these two things about myself:

    1. _____

    2. _____

I am_____.

(POSITIVE AFFIRMATION)

We must be aware that what we take in, is what we reflect out to the world. Make sure you are taking in things that make you feel love, gratitude, optimism, encouragement, hope, faith, and positivity. What you read, hear, and who you spend time with fills you and you always have a choice to control what comes in.

NeverStop.

I am grateful for these three things in my life

1. _____

2. _____

3. _____

I appreciate these two things about myself:

1. _____

2. _____

I am_____.

(POSITIVE AFFIRMATION)

We are all flawed but held together with good intentions. We will be wrong, and we will make mistakes, but we must do all things with good intentions. What we say and do matters but our intention behind it should always be clear. How we think, feel, and act matters. Be humble, do all things for good, and always choose love.

It takes more good intentions in the world to make a difference. We learn when we make mistakes but first, we must have good intentions.

NeverStop.

I am grateful for these three things in my life

1. _____

2. _____

3. _____

I appreciate these two things about myself:

1. _____

2. _____

I am_____.

(POSITIVE AFFIRMATION)

We need to learn that we need to ask for help sometimes. Never let your pride get in the way of your goals. People are brought into our lives for a purpose. Don't feel like you must do it alone because I am sure someone would love to show you love by helping you accomplish your goals. Asking for help is a sign of wisdom, not weakness.

We can accomplish a little by ourselves, but we can accomplish so much more with others. Alone we are strong, together we are unstoppable.

NeverStop.

I am grateful for these three things in my life

1. _____

2. _____

3. _____

I appreciate these two things about myself:

1. _____

2. _____

I am_____.

(POSITIVE AFFIRMATION)

We take the shape of the thoughts that we have most often. The people in your life should be making you better and bringing out the best in you. We take on the role that we have with the people we spend the most time with. Today, be a positive, encouraging, loving person that makes everyone around you better.

NeverStop.

I am grateful for these three things in my life

1. _____

2. _____

3. _____

I appreciate these two things about myself:

1. _____

2. _____

I am_____.
(POSITIVE AFFIRMATION)

Acting like we have every aspect of life figured out can get tiring. None of us have it all figured out. We learn and grow each day. Acting like we have everything together could prevent us from cultivating deep and honest relationships with people. No one expects you to be perfect so don't be anxious when you aren't; be humble.

It is ok to show vulnerability and humility. People will trust you more if they see that you are human just like everyone else. Be you, not who people think you should be.

NeverStop.

I am grateful for these three things in my life

1. _____

2. _____

3. _____

I appreciate these two things about myself:

1. _____

2. _____

I am_____.
(POSITIVE AFFIRMATION)

Find more joy in watching people succeed and seeing people feel their happiest. Find a way to support someone in a new way today. If we all encouraged one person, we would all be lifted higher. When you believe in people, it could inspire them to believe in themselves.

We must first be inspired to inspire others. Belief in one another is one of the most powerful things we can share with each other.

NeverStop.

I am grateful for these three things in my life

1. _____

2. _____

3. _____

I appreciate these two things about myself:

1. _____

2. _____

I am_____.
(POSITIVE AFFIRMATION)

We will all probably go through a tough time at some point in life. Let that connect all of us and bring us closer together. Be aware of opportunities for you to be there for others. Show love and support as often as possible. You never know when your heart and compassion can mean the world to someone.

Always know that everything you do matters to those around you. Your heart and energy can make a positive difference in people's lives.

NeverStop.

I am grateful for these three things in my life

1. _____

2. _____

3. _____

I appreciate these two things about myself:

1. _____

2. _____

I am_____.
(POSITIVE AFFIRMATION)

Don't get caught up comparing yourself to others. We are on a journey perfectly designed for each of us, and we likely don't know enough about other people to truly compare. Just measure yourself against your previous self and know that you can improve if you truly want to. Have faith and know you can, will, and must be your best.

Remain focused on how far you have come, not just how far you want to go. Have a clear picture of what you want and always remain positive and optimistic that you can make it a reality.

NeverStop.

I am grateful for these three things in my life

1. _____

2. _____

3. _____

I appreciate these two things about myself:

1. _____

2. _____

I am_____.

(POSITIVE AFFIRMATION)

Gratitude is a state of mind and a state of heart. It can change your life if you let it. Express gratitude as often as possible and slow down enough to feel gratitude as well. It affects our minds and leads to affecting our heart and our actions. Be grateful for what you have, not just the opportunity to have something become more.

Gratitude is the key to happiness. Deciding to be happy based on gratitude will allow you to maintain your sense of love, patience, faith, and hope.

NeverStop.

I am grateful for these three things in my life

1. _____

2. _____

3. _____

I appreciate these two things about myself:

1. _____

2. _____

I am_____.
(POSITIVE AFFIRMATION)

There is difference between being prepared for life and worrying sick about what could happen. We must acknowledge that some bad things might happen, but we have to be prepared. Keep your head down and focused on what is in front of you and learn to control what you can control. Focus on responsibility, not fault.

NeverStop.

I am grateful for these three things in my life

1. _____

2. _____

3. _____

I appreciate these two things about myself:

1. _____

2. _____

I am_____.

(POSITIVE AFFIRMATION)

Our minds are more powerful than we realize. We should learn how to use it and not be used by it. Our brains are constantly growing with each moment. What we tell ourselves will typically be what we will see. What our mind conceives, our body believes. Fill your mind more with "I Can" and positive affirmations.

The story we are telling ourselves is based on the past, learn to be present today and tell yourself a new type of inspiring message of your tomorrows. You can do amazing things.

NeverStop.

I am grateful for these three things in my life

1. _____

2. _____

3. _____

I appreciate these two things about myself:

1. _____

2. _____

I am_____.

(POSITIVE AFFIRMATION)

When you feel anxiety, let that be a cue that you need to stop and analyze things closely. We can often become anxious thinking about what could be and not necessarily, what is happening.

Being anxious could prevent us from seeing what is happening. Take a moment and reflect on the situation with a different perspective.

NeverStop.

I am grateful for these three things in my life

1. _____

2. _____

3. _____

I appreciate these two things about myself:

1. _____

2. _____

I am_____.
(POSITIVE AFFIRMATION)

Learn to unwind whenever possible. Rest in the presence of the current moment. These days, we need to unplug from our devices more than we are on them. We are created to need rest to become our best.

The direction we are going is more important than our speed. Always being on the go doesn't mean you are going in the right direction. Rest to focus, not to reconsider.

NeverStop.

I am grateful for these three things in my life

    1. _____

    2. _____

    3. _____

I appreciate these two things about myself:

    1. _____

    2. _____

I am_____.
(POSITIVE AFFIRMATION)

The world is full of different people and different points of view. Don't get stuck thinking the world needs to be your way. Cultivate an appreciation for the thoughts and beliefs of others, don't be threatened by them. We are made to be unique, not the same.

Appreciate the difference and similarities of the people in your life. Learning about their thoughts doesn't mean they have to become your thoughts. Always stay true to you.

NeverStop.

I am grateful for these three things in my life

    1. _____

    2. _____

    3. _____

I appreciate these two things about myself:

    1. _____

    2. _____

I am_____.
                              (POSITIVE AFFIRMATION)

No matter what is happening in your life, you can always find joy. Whether life seems easy, going great or life is challenging, and you feel like you are hanging on, find joy in both. You have been given each day and each opportunity on purpose and for a purpose. Your smile in those moments may inspire others.

Stay in control of your mindset and how you view the world. There is so much joy in this world.

NeverStop.

I am grateful for these three things in my life

1. _____

2. _____

3. _____

I appreciate these two things about myself:

1. _____

2. _____

I am_____.

(POSITIVE AFFIRMATION)

Never get caught up in the sense of entitlement. Hard work put in every day will give you a sense of pride and a feeling of earning what you are working for. Many things just seem given, but we should never take anything for granted. Just be grateful for everything you have whether you worked for it or not.

No matter what we have worked for or what we have been blessed with, let gratitude take over your heart and mind. Things come and go but we always get to choose our mindset.

NeverStop.

I am grateful for these three things in my life

1. _____

2. _____

3. _____

I appreciate these two things about myself:

1. _____

2. _____

I am_____.

(POSITIVE AFFIRMATION)

It's never too late to start making better and different decisions. Pursuing your purpose is a   moral obligation. Pursue what makes you excited to wake up every single day. Recognize when   your heart, mind, body, and soul feel alive and on fire.

If we are given the blessing of a day, we still have opportunities to pursue our purpose. Our   lives can change with each good decision we make. You will be glad you did when tomorrow   comes.

NeverStop.

I am grateful for these three things in my life

1. _____

2. _____

3. _____

I appreciate these two things about myself:

1. _____

2. _____

I am_____.

(POSITIVE AFFIRMATION)

What you don't know is more important than what you know. Be happy about learning opportunities, not threatened by them. Spend more time asking questions than you do proving that you are right. Keep your heart and your mind open.

Our ability to change, learn, and grow is a gift that each of us has been given. Be excited about opportunities to learn because those moments are preparing us for what is to come.

NeverStop.

I am grateful for these three things in my life

1. _____

2. _____

3. _____

I appreciate these two things about myself:

1. _____

2. _____

I am_____.
(POSITIVE AFFIRMATION)

Being in a new environment leads to sprit growth and brain growth. Demand more from yourself and trust your ability to endure. Be more courageous. Be more afraid of not doing something than doing it. Trust the path you are on and believe in yourself.

Seek out opportunities to become stronger, not more secure. Pursue growth, not comfort.

NeverStop.

I am grateful for these three things in my life

1. _____

2. _____

3. _____

I appreciate these two things about myself:

1. _____

2. _____

I am_____.

(POSITIVE AFFIRMATION)

It is very important to become someone that is easy to talk to. When other people trust you and your intentions, it will be easy for them to open up to you. Listen to understand, never judge, and don't interrupt people. When you listen, you are showing that you value the thoughts and opinions of others. Show love by listening and never judging anyone.

We have two ears and one mouth for a reason. Find joy in hearing about the lives of others. Cultivate relationships by listening.

NeverStop.

I am grateful for these three things in my life

    1. _____

    2. _____

    3. _____

I appreciate these two things about myself:

    1. _____

    2. _____

I am_____.
(POSITIVE AFFIRMATION)

Cultivate and recognize when your sprit is alive and thriving. Pay attention to what inspires you, makes you excited, and do more of those things. Appreciate your spirit because the people in your life already do.

NeverStop.

I am grateful for these three things in my life

1. _____

2. _____

3. _____

I appreciate these two things about myself:

1. _____

2. _____

I am_____.

(POSITIVE AFFIRMATION)

The power of belief is quite extraordinary. Our ability to believe in an outcome before we see it allows us to accomplish amazing things. Believe strongly in what you desire, and it will flow to you. Hold your belief until what you desire is realized. Believe you can and you will.

NeverStop.

I am grateful for these three things in my life

1. _____

2. _____

3. _____

I appreciate these two things about myself:

1. _____

2. _____

I am_____.
(POSITIVE AFFIRMATION)

Never let the opinions of others mean more to you than your opinion of yourself. What are you allowing to shape you right now? Take time each day to assess your daily habits and to determine a deeper sense of self. How others see you doesn't have to become your reality.
Always know you value. Shape your mind with your thoughts.

Never judge others and don't let the judgement of others affect you. That also means to not judge yourself. All of us are on a different journey that is meant just for us.

NeverStop.

I am grateful for these three things in my life

    1. _____

    2. _____

    3. _____

I appreciate these two things about myself:

    1. _____

    2. _____

I am_____.
(POSITIVE AFFIRMATION)

Sometimes it is tough to see what we need compared to what we have. Often, we use something not because we need it but because we have it. Quiet your mind to understand what is necessary for your heart and mind to be fulfilled. Live with a sense of fullness, not a sense of lack. Be grateful and be humble.

The difference between what we want and what we need is how we think about what we have. Need what you have, not what you want.

NeverStop.

I am grateful for these three things in my life

1. _____

2. _____

3. _____

I appreciate these two things about myself:

1. _____

2. _____

I am_____.

(POSITIVE AFFIRMATION)

Don't be ashamed of our failures, own them and learn from them. Don't be embarrassed by your success, learn from it and teach others what you have learned. Life is more about the matter of your heart during both experiences. Be hopeful be optimistic, be patient, and stay focused.

Success and failure should influence you in the same way. Be encouraged, learn, and grow.

NeverStop.

I am grateful for these three things in my life

1. _____

2. _____

3. _____

I appreciate these two things about myself:

1. _____

2. _____

I am_____.
(POSITIVE AFFIRMATION)

We need to keep life in balance. We need to share our gifts with others, but we must also let people share their gifts with us. Sometimes we need to say no to others so that we can say yes to ourselves. Taking care of your heart, mind, and body isn't being selfish...it is your responsibility and the only way you can be your best.

Keeping life in balance makes us stronger and makes us more ready for changes in life. Create balance, don't hope to find it.

NeverStop.

I am grateful for these three things in my life

1. _____

2. _____

3. _____

I appreciate these two things about myself:

1. _____

2. _____

I am_____.

(POSITIVE AFFIRMATION)

Take your guard down and let go of what you have been holding on to. Those are things that happened in the past and you must allow them to shape you and set them free. You can always be yourself and be made new. You deserve that just like everyone else does.

Focus on the goodness in life and know that you are meant to do great things in this world. Take life one day at a time but always remain grateful for yesterday, inspired today, and hopeful for tomorrow.

NeverStop.

I am grateful for these three things in my life

1. _____

2. _____

3. _____

I appreciate these two things about myself:

1. _____

2. _____

I am_____.

(POSITIVE AFFIRMATION)

Having an attitude of gratitude is a matter of the heart, not just the mind. Be inspired to help us live in a world where good people do good things for people without needing a thank you but we would still say thank you anyway. Happiness is the result of your attitude.

My life changed when my heart became full of gratitude. Find ways each day to cultivate gratitude in your heart and mind. It will change the way you look at what you have been blessed with.

NeverStop.

I am grateful for these three things in my life

1. _____

2. _____

3. _____

I appreciate these two things about myself:

1. _____

2. _____

I am_____.

(POSITIVE AFFIRMATION)

Let's be the change we want to see in the world. Show more kindness, humility, honesty, courage, compassion and be committed to your principles. The hearts of those around us are too good to lose faith in them. Just show the world something new because your heart and mind are just what it needs.

It's always the perfect time to do the right thing. We need to be role models for others, and we must lead by example. Listen to your heart and show it to the world.

NeverStop.

I am grateful for these three things in my life

1. _____

2. _____

3. _____

I appreciate these two things about myself:

1. _____

2. _____

I am_____.
(POSITIVE AFFIRMATION)

Humility and self-awareness are two things we should focus on to prevent our ego from taking over. It is hard to lead, motivate or make a difference if we cannot relate to other people. It is impossible to learn what we think we already know. Learn to appreciate the impact of humbling moments in life.

Never let your ego be a strong force in your life. No matter our abilities, we will all have opportunities to improve. Relate, connect, be humble and love on others.

NeverStop.

I am grateful for these three things in my life

1. _____

2. _____

3. _____

I appreciate these two things about myself:

1. _____

2. _____

I am_____.
(POSITIVE AFFIRMATION)

Everyone needs love. Everyone needs respect. Everyone needs dignity. Everyone needs honor. Everyone includes you. Always remember your value and what you deserve. Putting others first is noble but you should still make time for yourself. Make time to take care of your heart, mind, and body. Those around you need you to show yourself that love. Never forget others but always remember yourself.

Find ways each day to take time for yourself. Loving to give is great if we have habits that fill our heart and mind with love, fulfillment, and gratitude.

NeverStop.

I am grateful for these three things in my life

1. _____

2. _____

3. _____

I appreciate these two things about myself:

1. _____

2. _____

I am_____.

(POSITIVE AFFIRMATION)

Love people in unexpected ways. Be kind when it could be easy to be angry. Be generous when you have very little. Be grateful when you are being guided through troubled waters. Love is a natural feeling for us. Stay in control of your heart and mind.

Love can be shown in a variety of ways. Look for opportunities to show love when others don't expect it. Some of the best things in life are unexpected.

NeverStop.

I am grateful for these three things in my life

1. _____

2. _____

3. _____

I appreciate these two things about myself:

1. _____

2. _____

I am_____.

(POSITIVE AFFIRMATION)

Be willing to try new things and enjoy the process of getting to know yourself. Seek fulfillment more than comfort. Study yourself more than you study the lives of others. Appreciate what makes you feel joy and grateful and slow down enough in those moments to create a feeling that you will always remember.

Pay attention to the moments that bring you joy and make the effort to create more of those moments in your life. Our decisions determine our direction.

NeverStop.

I am grateful for these three things in my life

1. _____

2. _____

3. _____

I appreciate these two things about myself:

1. _____

2. _____

I am_____.
(POSITIVE AFFIRMATION)

The list of things to be grateful for goes beyond what we can see. Be grateful for how you feel and for things you can't see with your eyes, but you can feel it. When someone loves you or shows compassion, be grateful. When your challenges end up being the exact thing you needed to transform your heart and mind, be grateful. Look for good things happening to you and for you.

Experience life with all of your senses to gain an understanding of gratitude for everything you have in this life. Life is for you, not against you.

NeverStop.

I am grateful for these three things in my life

1. _____

2. _____

3. _____

I appreciate these two things about myself:

1. _____

2. _____

I am_____.
(POSITIVE AFFIRMATION)

In times of trouble or crisis, it is best to stop, get your bearings, calm yourself, take a breath, and then proceed. Learn how to respond to adversity instead of reacting to it. Act quickly but don't be in a hurry. We make our best decisions when we are in control of our mind. Keep your head up and heart open and always have faith.

We always have a choice about how we let challenges affect us. My suggestion, be inspired and focused and trust that challenges are helping you become who you are meant to be.

NeverStop.

I am grateful for these three things in my life

1. _____

2. _____

3. _____

I appreciate these two things about myself:

1. _____

2. _____

I am_____.

(POSITIVE AFFIRMATION)

One lesson I have learned is that the little things end up being the big things. Those little efforts every single day add up to be the biggest inspiration to ourselves and to others. Do what you can, where you are, with everything that you have. You can make a massive impact on the world when you use your gifts. The world needs you to be you.

Always do what you can to help others and know that whatever you can do is always enough. It is the state of our heart that matters the most, not how much you give.

NeverStop.

I am grateful for these three things in my life

1. _____

2. _____

3. _____

I appreciate these two things about myself:

1. _____

2. _____

I am_____.

(POSITIVE AFFIRMATION)

Life changes once you realize we are all in this together. You don't have to succeed at the expense of others losing, there are enough opportunities for all of us to win. Choose to show more love and help others success around you as much as possible. Our differences make us stronger, not weaker.

Don't feel like you must fit in to be accepted. We are uniquely made to complement each other, not be the same as everyone else. You are enough just as you are right now.

NeverStop.

I am grateful for these three things in my life

1. _____
2. _____
3. _____

I appreciate these two things about myself:

1. _____
2. _____

I am_____.
(POSITIVE AFFIRMATION)

Life is full of moments that can take our breath away if we just quiet our mind enough to let it happen. Today, I encourage you to slow down and recognize the beauty of this world and be grateful for the moment that was designed for you. Don't get caught up in the next thing when you haven't yet truly appreciated what you currently have right in front of you.

Each day is full of moments that can make an impact on us for a lifetime, but we have to slow down enough to recognize them.

NeverStop.

I am grateful for these three things in my life

1. _____

2. _____

3. _____

I appreciate these two things about myself:

1. _____

2. _____

I am_____.

(POSITIVE AFFIRMATION)

We tend to spend energy judging ourselves based on how we look or feel. We must use that same energy for self-love and recognizing all the great things we have to offer. There is a big difference between self-reflecting and judgment. Look at yourself like you look at others and always see the best in other people.

Learn to love yourselves with the same love you give to others. You must first know that you are loved before you can fully love others.

NeverStop.

I am grateful for these three things in my life

1. _____

2. _____

3. _____

I appreciate these two things about myself:

1. _____

2. _____

I am_____.

(POSITIVE AFFIRMATION)

Be grateful where you are. Have faith that even more great things are coming your way. Moments come and go but how we allow them to make us feel will last forever. Celebrate the blessings and overcome the challenges. Breathe. Smile. Relax. Enjoy. Enjoy the paradise around you.

Happiness begins with gratitude. How we think of the world will make us see the world differently.

NeverStop.

I am grateful for these three things in my life

1. _____

2. _____

3. _____

I appreciate these two things about myself:

1. _____

2. _____

I am_____.

(POSITIVE AFFIRMATION)

We put a lot of effort in determining what is urgent and what is not. We also put a lot of effort into planning or taking time making "when I" lists or bucket lists. Be careful because life will go by fast and we never have as much time as we think we do. We don't have forever but we do have today. Live your life to the fullest and be present in each moment.

Have a strategy, not just a plan. We never know what each day will bring so plans might have to change. Be prepared for what could happen while remaining optimistic.

NeverStop.

I am grateful for these three things in my life

1. _____

2. _____

3. _____

I appreciate these two things about myself:

1. _____

2. _____

I am_____.
(POSITIVE AFFIRMATION)

We are not stuck in time. We all have the ability to learn more. Today, make it a point to go out and learn instead of waiting for someone to teach you. Be humble enough to know and say that you don't know everything. When you learn something, share it with multiple people, do it with simplicity, and never boast.

We learn more when we are listening, not talking. Welcome new insights and information into your mind and let it affect your heart. You will never go back.

NeverStop.

I am grateful for these three things in my life

1. _____

2. _____

3. _____

I appreciate these two things about myself:

1. _____

2. _____

I am_____.
(POSITIVE AFFIRMATION)

Don't be scared or threatened to change and improve your life. You deserve to improve your life without judgement. One small change in your life could be the thing that changes every aspect of your life. Pay attention to the tugs on your heart and the things you think about most often. You should likely pursue those things.

Don't get caught up in seeking the approval of others when it comes to pursuing the desires you have on your heart. They are your desires, not theirs. Believe in yourself and stay focused on your purpose.

NeverStop.

I am grateful for these three things in my life

1. _____

2. _____

3. _____

I appreciate these two things about myself:

1. _____

2. _____

I am_____.

(POSITIVE AFFIRMATION)

Never be afraid to be your true self. Your uniqueness may just be the beauty we have been looking for. Don't get caught up trying to fit in, we are meant to complement each other. Love what make you special.

Be true to yourself. Seek to understand and appreciate yourself just as much as you do others.

NeverStop.

I am grateful for these three things in my life

    1. _____

    2. _____

    3. _____

I appreciate these two things about myself:

    1. _____

    2. _____

I am_____.

                              (POSITIVE AFFIRMATION)

Don't measure the day by how long it is. You will always have, minutes in a day. Instead, measure the day by its depth. Measure it by the lessons learned, challenges overcome, and the limitations surpassed. That is when you find fulfillment daily. Be grateful for each day and remain optimistic.

Our ability to change, learn, grow is a gift that each of us has been given. Be excited about opportunities to learn because those moments are preparing us for what is to come.

NeverStop.

I am grateful for these three things in my life

1. _____

2. _____

3. _____

I appreciate these two things about myself:

1. _____

2. _____

I am_____.

(POSITIVE AFFIRMATION)

If you have a desire on your heart to make a change or if you know you should take action... just start. Stop putting it off. Take the initiative to take the first step. Believe you can and you will. Trust that you already have the strength it takes and get out of your own way.

We are given the gift of opportunity and a fresh start each day. Be inspired by your vision and never let your past hold you back.

NeverStop.

I am grateful for these three things in my life

1. _____

2. _____

3. _____

I appreciate these two things about myself:

1. _____

2. _____

I am_____.
(POSITIVE AFFIRMATION)

Cultivate love and seek common ground and solutions. We all feel happier when we show and receive love. Love can look like kindness, patience, humility, gifts, acts of service, quality time, or words of affirmation. We all show and receive love in a unique way. Look for it and you will find more of it. Hope you find it today!

NeverStop.

I am grateful for these three things in my life

1. _____

2. _____

3. _____

I appreciate these two things about myself:

1. _____

2. _____

I am_____.
(POSITIVE AFFIRMATION)

It is easy to get distracted by the fast pace of life and it can be hard to find time to maintain the process of improving your mind and body. Don't let the fact that you can't do all that you planned to do prevent you from doing anything at all. Small progress is always better than standing still. Create small wins to cultivate momentum.

Do all that you can and be patient with yourself. Doing your best is a matter of your heart and mind. Focus on progress, not perfection.

NeverStop.

I am grateful for these three things in my life

1. _____

2. _____

3. _____

I appreciate these two things about myself:

1. _____

2. _____

I am_____.
        (POSITIVE AFFIRMATION)

Find the balance between indulging and resisting. Just become more aware of your heart and mind and see your habits more clearly. There is a beautiful rhythm to life it shouldn't always feel like a battle or push and pull. Once you understand that you control your daily habits, you are able to appreciate the rhythm without having it negatively impact your state of mind.

NeverStop.

I am grateful for these three things in my life

1. _____

2. _____

3. _____

I appreciate these two things about myself:

1. _____

2. _____

I am_____.
(POSITIVE AFFIRMATION)

Discipline comes from having a clear vision. When we start with a clear goal in mind, the work shifts from stress to passion. If you lose momentum, don't change the vision but change your strategy. We are a product of our daily habits so make sure they are helping you. Clear your mind. Focus on the vision. Believe.

Discipline is the difference between what you want now and what you want to the most.

NeverStop.

I am grateful for these three things in my life

    1. _____

    2. _____

    3. _____

I appreciate these two things about myself:

    1. _____

    2. _____

I am_____.

                               (POSITIVE AFFIRMATION)

If you live a life of focusing on getting things, you will only be happy when you get those things. If you focus your life on giving, you will always be filled with joy because you will continually see your impact on others. Seek lifelong fulfilment, not just instant gratification.

NeverStop.

I am grateful for these three things in my life

1. _____

2. _____

3. _____

I appreciate these two things about myself:

1. _____

2. _____

I am_____.
(POSITIVE AFFIRMATION)

Keep your focus on who you are and where you are going. Even if you can't see the entire road in front of you, it just takes faith that you are being guided on purpose for a purpose. You have all of the light inside of you to see as far as you need to. The vision of your future should go beyond what you see in front of you. Be courageous, be bold, and pursue your purpose.

NeverStop.

I am grateful for these three things in my life

1. _____

2. _____

3. _____

I appreciate these two things about myself:

1. _____

2. _____

I am_____.

(POSITIVE AFFIRMATION)

We like to make lists because it makes us feel like we are making progress and accomplishing something. Spend more time on your gratitude list that you do on your to-do list. In the end, the gratitude list will always mean more to us and those are the things we wish we had more of. Be overflowed with gratitude and share that with others. Develop daily gratitude habits and it will change your outlook on this amazing life.

Once you focus more on what you have than what you want, you will realize you have everything you need. Gratitude leads to happiness.

NeverStop.

I am grateful for these three things in my life

1. _____

2. _____

3. _____

I appreciate these two things about myself:

1. _____

2. _____

I am_____.

(POSITIVE AFFIRMATION)

Our lives are a reflection of what we believe to be true about ourselves. What we believe, we will experience. What we experience, we will believe. Spend your life looking for things that bring you joy; they will keep finding you as well. Daily affirmations are the key to unlocking self- awareness. You are valuable, blessed, and loved beyond measure.

Believe that you deserve the great things that are coming your way. Not because you have done something great but because that has been the plan all along. Have faith.

NeverStop.

I am grateful for these three things in my life

1. _____

2. _____

3. _____

I appreciate these two things about myself:

1. _____

2. _____

I am_____.

(POSITIVE AFFIRMATION)

Accept everyone unconditionally while still encouraging people to be better. Show love and never judge anyone. There is a big difference between making people like they can be more versus what they have to be. We each have the gift of inspiring others if we lead with our heart.

See people as they could be and they will start acting like they should be. Inspire and encourage with all of your heart.

NeverStop.

I am grateful for these three things in my life

1. _____

2. _____

3. _____

I appreciate these two things about myself:

1. _____

2. _____

I am_____.

(POSITIVE AFFIRMATION)

Our mind gets nourished when we test our physical capabilities. Working on your brain should be complemented with raining your body. Get lost in exercise. Sometimes we cannot think our way out of a thinking problem. The brain will likely concede way before the body does. Push your body to renew your mind.

Always know that our bodies and minds can improve. It's never too late to start. Invest in yourself daily.

NeverStop.

I am grateful for these three things in my life

    1. _____

    2. _____

    3. _____

I appreciate these two things about myself:

    1. _____

    2. _____

I am_____.

(POSITIVE AFFIRMATION)

We will make mistakes. We must find a way to forgive ourselves. Use your mistakes; don't let your mistakes use you. No one is perfect. No one needs you to be perfect. Keep your head up and heart soft and believe that each moment is preparing you for the next. Your persistence is inspiring.

Don't let mistakes distract you, they should be used to focus you. We will keep being taught a lesson until we have learned it.

NeverStop.

I am grateful for these three things in my life

1. _____

2. _____

3. _____

I appreciate these two things about myself:

1. _____

2. _____

I am_____.
(POSITIVE AFFIRMATION)

Gratitude is the catalyst to a positive and optimistic mindset. Be content with what you have, and you will receive more to enjoy. Being content isn't settling, it is more that you are settled and at peace with your current chapter of life. Find abundant joy in what you have been blessed with. That will open your heart and mind to receive things that are even more amazing.

Be so full of gratitude that you begin to forget about what you don't have and just focus on the amazing blessings you have in your life. Write down three things each morning... be patient... be real... the transformation is amazing.

NeverStop.

I am grateful for these three things in my life

1. _____

2. _____

3. _____

I appreciate these two things about myself:

1. _____

2. _____

I am_____.

(POSITIVE AFFIRMATION)

Never ignore a call to action. Do what you feel you are compelled to do. That energy and that opportunity has been perfectly created for you. Create a crystal-clear vision and focus on your why. If something challenging comes up, the answer is to just keep doing it. Work on yourself, be patient, and be transformed.

Don't get caught up in waiting for the perfect time to pursue what you are passionate about. Every moment in life is preparing us for the next.

NeverStop.

I am grateful for these three things in my life

1. _____

2. _____

3. _____

I appreciate these two things about myself:

1. _____

2. _____

I am_____.

(POSITIVE AFFIRMATION)

We should all try to encourage and inspire people but sometimes we need to simply seek to understand how people are actually feeling. Be compassionate and present in your conversations because people will tell you more when you actually listen. We have two ears and one mouth for a reason. Love the process of getting to know the people in your life.

Show others that you value them by the way you listen to them. Your attention and effort matters in every moment.

NeverStop.

I am grateful for these three things in my life

1. _____

2. _____

3. _____

I appreciate these two things about myself:

1. _____

2. _____

I am_____.

(POSITIVE AFFIRMATION)

Whatever comes our way, we always have a choice. Choose to be the best of yourself. It's the choices we make that make us who are. We can always choose to do what is right and what is good. Even if it is tough in the moment, you always have a choice. You are strong, capable, and significant. Be good, kind, loving, patient, and hopeful.

Our choices today affect our tomorrows. Our actions are a reflection of what we want. Make sure your choices reflect who you really are.

NeverStop.

I am grateful for these three things in my life

    1. _____

    2. _____

    3. _____

I appreciate these two things about myself:

    1. _____

    2. _____

I am_____.

                      (POSITIVE AFFIRMATION)

Don't spend one second of your life with revenge or regret in your heart. Feeling those things doesn't do us any good. The thing to do is let go and move on to positive thoughts that encourage you. Life is too short to have any other feelings than love, gratitude, and optimism. Being at your best starts with a clear mind that you are in control of.

Your heart and mind are way too valuable to get caught up in negative thoughts. Cultivate self- awareness to be able to recognize when you have these thoughts and move on quickly.

NeverStop.

I am grateful for these three things in my life

    1. _____

    2. _____

    3. _____

I appreciate these two things about myself:

    1. _____

    2. _____

I am_____.

                      (POSITIVE AFFIRMATION)

As the sun reaches out to the moon with beautiful light, you should also reach for what you desire. When we reach, we stretch, and we discover that we are able to do more than we thought. You may be surprised to find that what you are seeking is within your reach. Challenge yourself and shine your light… you just might find what you have been looking for.

Reach for the moon because even if you fall short, you are still in the starts. Believe in the strength inside of you and reach today.

NeverStop.

I am grateful for these three things in my life

1. _____

2. _____

3. _____

I appreciate these two things about myself:

1. _____

2. _____

I am_____.

(POSITIVE AFFIRMATION)

We must learn the difference between taking a rest to focus and stopping because you are losing focus. Momentum is so important on the path to success and accomplishing your goals. So, no matter what, always remember that we just need to show up each day, trust in the process, and focus on why you started.

Take time to rest but never stop focusing on your goal.

NeverStop.

I am grateful for these three things in my life

1. _____

2. _____

3. _____

I appreciate these two things about myself:

1. _____

2. _____

I am_____.

(POSITIVE AFFIRMATION)

Set goals and develop strategies like an adult but believe and imagine like a child. Your self- limiting beliefs are not real; they are false impressions of who you used to be. Believe in the amazing, fulfilling road ahead. Have steadfast faith in the perfect timing of life and know the world is for you.

Have the belief and imagination of a child to set huge goals for yourself. Believe you can and you will!

NeverStop.

I am grateful for these three things in my life

1. _____

2. _____

3. _____

I appreciate these two things about myself:

1. _____

2. _____

I am_____.

(POSITIVE AFFIRMATION)

Equality in opportunity doesn't mean equality in outcome. Just because we have the resources, doesn't mean we will use them to the fullest. Out effort determines our direction. That should be inspiring, not heavy. Control what you can... your effort and attitude. You never know, your outcome might be better than anything you have imagined.

Give great effort and have a positive mindset. Your future may be even better than you planned.

NeverStop.

I am grateful for these three things in my life

    1. _____

    2. _____

    3. _____

I appreciate these two things about myself:

    1. _____

    2. _____

I am_____.

(POSITIVE AFFIRMATION)

Each day is a new day full of opportunities to contribute to each other. You contribute to others with your words, effort, and actions. Even if you aren't trying to, you can influence others. Just decide to contribute great things into people's lives and be a positive, encouraging, empowering influence in their life. See people as they could be and they will begin to act as they should be.

Be someone that adds to people's lives, not takes. Your heart and mind have the ability to energize and influence others.

NeverStop.

I am grateful for these three things in my life

1. _____

2. _____

3. _____

I appreciate these two things about myself:

1. _____

2. _____

I am_____.
(POSITIVE AFFIRMATION)

Focus on celebrating who you are and less on analyzing what you are not. Get off the "fix me" cycle... you are not broken. You are just putting the pieces together to become who you have always meant to be. Be optimistic and hopeful.

You can't find value by digging into your faults. No one is perfect but we have the choice to become our best.

NeverStop.

I am grateful for these three things in my life

1. _____

2. _____

3. _____

I appreciate these two things about myself:

1. _____

2. _____

I am_____.

(POSITIVE AFFIRMATION)

If you want to make a difference in the world, you have to invest even more time in your own personal transformation. When you are rested, healthy, grateful, inspired, and focused, you are able to be at your best when others need you. Never put yourself second because we need you at your best. You are worth it. It is showing yourself love, not being selfish.

Take time and make time for your heart, mind, and body. We are never too busy to love and   care for ourselves.

NeverStop.

I am grateful for these three things in my life

1. _____

2. _____

3. _____

I appreciate these two things about myself:

1. _____

2. _____

I am_____.
(POSITIVE AFFIRMATION)

Don't rely on crossing your fingers or good luck charms to get you to where you want to be. The more effort you give, the luckier you will get. Good breaks will find you when your effort has placed in the right opportunity. Luck shouldn't be your strategy. Luck isn't by chance; it is typically the result of choices you made to take action in life. Be bod. Be strong.

All of your good fortune has always been planned for you. Trust fate more than luck.

NeverStop.

I am grateful for these three things in my life

1. _____

2. _____

3. _____

I appreciate these two things about myself:

1. _____

2. _____

I am_____.

(POSITIVE AFFIRMATION)

Find the balance of being patient while fully utilizing every moment of your life. Don't rush everything just to get a result. The best things come out of the oven, not the microwave. Be willing to put in the time and effort to get the results you actually want. Be optimistic and relentless.

Use every moment you are blessed with to become who you have been created to be.

NeverStop.

I am grateful for these three things in my life

1. _____

2. _____

3. _____

I appreciate these two things about myself:

1. _____

2. _____

I am_____.

(POSITIVE AFFIRMATION)

Cultivate the skill of focus. When we try to focus, we often try to think really hard. That is the mistake and why it rarely works. Try to think less when you are needing to focus and just let your mind and body take over. Focus on breathing, not the task at hand. Sometimes we just need to get out of our own way. You will discover a new level of performance.

Being able to focus is a skill we must learn. Use your mind, don't let it use you.

NeverStop.

I am grateful for these three things in my life

1. _____

2. _____

3. _____

I appreciate these two things about myself:

1. _____

2. _____

I am_____.
(POSITIVE AFFIRMATION)

If you are working on creating better habits and raising your standards, just be patient. In the beginning, you have to demand a lot from your mind and body. In time, your mind and body will begin to demand it of you because it wants to maintain your new standard. Don't rush something you want to last forever.
Great things take time. Put in the effort and remember why you started.

NeverStop.

I am grateful for these three things in my life

1. _____

2. _____

3. _____

I appreciate these two things about myself:

1. _____

2. _____

I am_____.
(POSITIVE AFFIRMATION)

If you help others, we all win. It's important to slow down and realize how much we all have in common and how connected we all are. Being kind and generous to others ids the most rewarding thing you can do. Make a purposeful effort to do something kind for someone today. Encourage others to do good for others. Be love.

Everything affects everything else. Use your words and actions to spread goodness and gratitude.

NeverStop.

I am grateful for these three things in my life

1. _____

2. _____

3. _____

I appreciate these two things about myself:

1. _____

2. _____

I am_____.

(POSITIVE AFFIRMATION)

Live each day to the fullest. Not like it is your last day but as if it could be. Don't spend too much time being concerned about the future or maintaining your past. We never know how many days we have left but we do know that we have today. Enjoy the blessing of life you have been given. Cherish every moment. Fill each day with things that make you feel loved, inspired, and grateful.

NeverStop.

I am grateful for these three things in my life

1. _____

2. _____

3. _____

I appreciate these two things about myself:

1. _____

2. _____

I am_____.
(POSITIVE AFFIRMATION)

We give power to the things we think about and talk about. Give your energy, thoughts, and words to gratitude, optimism, love, and positivity. Feed those things with your energy by looking for them, talking about them and looking like them. We will find what we are looking for. Use your energy for goodness.

Be so full of gratitude, love, optimism, and positivity that you don't have room for anything else.

NeverStop.

I am grateful for these three things in my life

1. _____

2. _____

3. _____

I appreciate these two things about myself:

1. _____

2. _____

I am_____.

(POSITIVE AFFIRMATION)

The way we respond to event or people in our livers is based on a habit. We develop a habit of reacting to things in life and that is when anger and frustration takes over our hearts and minds. Acknowledge your freedom to make a new habit, make a new way to respond. Choose to: forgive, love, be patient, be grateful, laugh, and smile.

Remain in control of your heart and mind. Don't give the control to others.

NeverStop.

I am grateful for these three things in my life

1. _____

2. _____

3. _____

I appreciate these two things about myself:

1. _____

2. _____

I am_____.

(POSITIVE AFFIRMATION)

Always remember how fortunate, lucky, and blessed you are. Don't let a moment of misfortune shift your mindset to a life of bad luck. Look at the bigger picture, gain a better perspective, and always know how important it is for you to endure and persevere. We have a lot going for us so pay attention to those things in your life.

Maintain an attitude of gratitude and optimism in moments of misfortune.

NeverStop.

I am grateful for these three things in my life

1. _____

2. _____

3. _____

I appreciate these two things about myself:

1. _____

2. _____

I am_____.

(POSITIVE AFFIRMATION)

We must learn to worry less. Life is not in alignment with our worries. Life is way more unexpected and is much more factual. After the moment passes, we find out we didn't need to be worried, or we have been worrying about the wrong thing. So let go, trust in the plan, and know that you have great things coming for you. Our plan may be unknown but how we respond is always in our control.

Do not be afraid. Be free from fear, trust with all of your heart.

NeverStop.

I am grateful for these three things in my life

1. _____

2. _____

3. _____

I appreciate these two things about myself:

1. _____

2. _____

I am_____.

(POSITIVE AFFIRMATION)

Challenge yourself to dedicate the rest of this year to self-mastery, self-discipline, and self- actualization. The time will pass anyway so you might as well use every minute to the fullest. You will be glad you did and world need you too. Today is a great day to begin the journey that is meant just for you. Just decide... make the rest of your life, the best of your life.

Live life to the fullest and demand the most from yourself for the rest of the year. Create sustainable standards and see the amazing transformation that happens.

NeverStop.

I am grateful for these three things in my life

1. _____

2. _____

3. _____

I appreciate these two things about myself:

1. _____

2. _____

I am_____.

(POSITIVE AFFIRMATION)

Don't be convenient with your compassion. We all have the capacity to be compassionate when someone needs our help. We should be that compassionate all of the time since it only takes a choice. Compassion is not something that has to be taught; it is who we are when our thoughts are clear. How we think about things will always dictate how we treat them.

The time to be compassionate is now. Be kind, not just nice.

NeverStop.

I am grateful for these three things in my life

1. _____

2. _____

3. _____

I appreciate these two things about myself:

1. _____

2. _____

I am_____.
(POSITIVE AFFIRMATION)

Resist the negative thoughts that lead to a sense of lack, of drama and blame. That's not really who you are and those thoughts are just distracting you. Affirm the thoughts of abundance, responsibility, compassion, and hope. That is the truth of our hearts and minds that need to be set free.

The time to be compassionate is now. Be kind, not just nice.

NeverStop.

I am grateful for these three things in my life

1. _____

2. _____

3. _____

I appreciate these two things about myself:

1. _____

2. _____

I am_____.

(POSITIVE AFFIRMATION)

Our mindset determines our direction. There might be moments that make you feel like you have lost your way, but with the right optimistic positive mindset, you know that you are merely finding your way and you are on the right path to where you are meant to be.

Trust that your path is meant to shape you, not break you.

NeverStop.

I am grateful for these three things in my life

1. _____

2. _____

3. _____

I appreciate these two things about myself:

1. _____

2. _____

I am_____.

(POSITIVE AFFIRMATION)

A challenging time or sad time is just for now; remain hopeful. Happiness and joy may also be just for now; remain grateful. We are all one moment or one decision away from a different life. Don't live in fear of what might happen because you could be missing the amazing things that actually are happening in your life.

I hope you have a day full of moments that inspire and encourage you. Make today a great day.

NeverStop.

I am grateful for these three things in my life

1. _____

2. _____

3. _____

I appreciate these two things about myself:

1. _____

2. _____

I am_____.
(POSITIVE AFFIRMATION)

Never underestimate the impact of mindful breathing. Luckily, we have been created to do it without thought to sustain life. However, when we calm our mind enough to breathe on purpose and with intent it transforms our state of mind, alter our chemistry, and prepares our body to perform at its highest level. Inhale gratitude and courage and exhale fears and burdens. Slow down and take a deep breath. Focus on a calm heart, mind, and body.

Take time to thank people for being you and for making a difference in my world.

NeverStop.

I am grateful for these three things in my life

1. _____

2. _____

3. _____

I appreciate these two things about myself:

1. _____

2. _____

I am_____.
(POSITIVE AFFIRMATION)

The difference between what you expected and what you received is what you actually needed. Be encouraged by all that you already have. Don't be let down by not getting what you expected, cultivate steadfast gratitude for even having the opportunity to receive anything at all. Need what you have, not what you want. Be optimistic and hopeful.

NeverStop.

I am grateful for these three things in my life

1. _____

2. _____

3. _____

I appreciate these two things about myself:

1. _____

2. _____

I am_____.
(POSITIVE AFFIRMATION)

Control what we can and let go of what we can't. Don't rely on recognition from others. That is outside of your control. Don't let your happiness due to recognition depend on others. It's called self-esteem not other's esteem. Do what you know is right and never need the credit from others.

NeverStop.

I am grateful for these three things in my life

1. _____

2. _____

3. _____

I appreciate these two things about myself:

1. _____

2. _____

I am_____.

(POSITIVE AFFIRMATION)

It is so important that we learn to care about each other. We were made for each other. Keep your eyes on the good things happening because it is tough to make a positive difference when you are in despair. Stay focused on goodness so you can reflect that good energy back to the world. Be optimistic. Be humble.

NeverStop.

I am grateful for these three things in my life

    1. _____

    2. _____

    3. _____

I appreciate these two things about myself:

    1. _____

    2. _____

I am_____.
                      (POSITIVE AFFIRMATION)

Be humble enough to know that you aren't better than anyone else but be wise enough to know that you are different from the ret. We each have gifts but what we do with our gifts makes us unique and stand out. Do more than you have to and unleash your potential.

NeverStop.

I am grateful for these three things in my life

1. _____

2. _____

3. _____

I appreciate these two things about myself:

1. _____

2. _____

I am_____.

(POSITIVE AFFIRMATION)

As long as we are working and training our mind and body the best we can do, that is all we can do. Always know that your effort matters in every moment. Give all that you have and you will see you have a little more in you. Push yourself beyond your previous limitations.

NeverStop.

I am grateful for these three things in my life

1. _____

2. _____

3. _____

I appreciate these two things about myself:

1. _____

2. _____

I am_____.
(POSITIVE AFFIRMATION)

There is a time for fast improvement and there is a time for vast improvement. Recognize your fast improvements to sustain your vast improvements and always maintain your highest standards. Be patient with yourself and be patient with the perfect timing of life.

NeverStop.

I am grateful for these three things in my life

1. _____

2. _____

3. _____

I appreciate these two things about myself:

1. _____

2. _____

I am_____.
(POSITIVE AFFIRMATION)

Greatness doesn't worry about being great, it just keeps on working to improve, to become the best. Keep your focus forward.

NeverStop.

I am grateful for these three things in my life

1. _____

2. _____

3. _____

I appreciate these two things about myself:

1. _____

2. _____

I am_____.

(POSITIVE AFFIRMATION)

Life come at us pretty fast. It can all change in one instant. Things can be added or removed from our lives without a known reason. We must remain steadfast in our hope, faith, and love. Be prepared for the twists and turns that are meant to shape you, not break you. Look for the light in your life, not the shadows.

NeverStop.

I am grateful for these three things in my life

1. _____

2. _____

3. _____

I appreciate these two things about myself:

1. _____

2. _____

I am_____.
(POSITIVE AFFIRMATION)

Have the courage to take responsibility for yourself. The courage to resist the status quo and the desire to "fit in." Plus, we need to have the courage to stand up for what's right. When optimism and courage are present, hope still remains. Trust in your purpose and your ability to make a positive change in your life. Be bold, be kind, be courageous.

NeverStop.

I am grateful for these three things in my life

1. _____

2. _____

3. _____

I appreciate these two things about myself:

1. _____

2. _____

I am_____.
(POSITIVE AFFIRMATION)

Real strength doesn't mean you are free from fear. It is about knowing it intimately and moving beyond it. We are able to learn how strong we are only when we are forced to endure and withstand and when we must be strong. Trust in the strength inside of you to carry you through fear.

NeverStop.

I am grateful for these three things in my life

1. _____

2. _____

3. _____

I appreciate these two things about myself:

1. _____

2. _____

I am_____.
(POSITIVE AFFIRMATION)

Our mindset determines our direction. Do more and give more effort because you want to be better, not because you aren't good enough as you are. Trust that you are right where you are meant to be in every single moment but when you feel that pull in your heart, challenge yourself in the open waters and trust in your gifts.

NeverStop.

I am grateful for these three things in my life

1. _____

2. _____

3. _____

I appreciate these two things about myself:

1. _____

2. _____

I am_____.

(POSITIVE AFFIRMATION)

We must always be respectful even if we aren't treated with the proper respect. How we treat everyone matters and it is a reflection of our character. Always be polite, forgiving, tolerant, and stay in control of your thoughts and actions. Respond in a way that you won't regret.

NeverStop.

I am grateful for these three things in my life

1. _____

2. _____

3. _____

I appreciate these two things about myself:

1. _____

2. _____

I am_____.
(POSITIVE AFFIRMATION)

We must cultivate the skill of self-control and self-discipline. Once we realize that we control our desires and we have the ability to instantly change the way we think about things, we will begin to focus on what we want, not what we don't want.

NeverStop.

I am grateful for these three things in my life

1. _____

2. _____

3. _____

I appreciate these two things about myself:

1. _____

2. _____

I am_____.
(POSITIVE AFFIRMATION)

We must be aware of the dangers of our immediate, emotional reactions to events since these split second judgements are often based on an unclear view. When things happen, don't go with your first opinion based on your initial reaction. Just quickly pause and you will likely see things in a new way. Respond more that you react.

NeverStop.

I am grateful for these three things in my life

1. _____

2. _____

3. _____

I appreciate these two things about myself:

1. _____

2. _____

I am_____.
(POSITIVE AFFIRMATION)

Be modest and succinct in your words but bold and exceed expectations with your actions. Your actions are a reflection of your heart. Talk gets you started but actions get you finished. Do more and say less. Be honest, be kind, be bold, be humble.

NeverStop.

I am grateful for these three things in my life

1. _____

2. _____

3. _____

I appreciate these two things about myself:

1. _____

2. _____

I am_____.
(POSITIVE AFFIRMATION)

As a humankind, we have two important tasks:
1. To be human... not perfect, not without flaws or imperfections, but human.
2. We are meant to be kind... to ourselves and to each other. Start there, be the change, be optimistic.

NeverStop.

I am grateful for these three things in my life

1. _____

2. _____

3. _____

I appreciate these two things about myself:

1. _____

2. _____

I am_____.

(POSITIVE AFFIRMATION)

Sometimes being still is a display of strength, focus and preparation for taking action. Don't always feel like you have to be moving in order to be prepared for taking action. Being still allows your heart, mind, and body to be in the best state to take the best action, not just any action.

NeverStop.

I am grateful for these three things in my life

1. _____

2. _____

3. _____

I appreciate these two things about myself:

1. _____

2. _____

I am_____.
(POSITIVE AFFIRMATION)

How long are you going to wait before you demand the best from yourself? We aren't born lazy, we just have to be refocused on our purpose. There is a difference between being lazy and mindfully resting. Resting is recharging to take action and being lazy is not understanding the importance to taking action. It's simply making a choice.

NeverStop.

I am grateful for these three things in my life

1. _____

2. _____

3. _____

I appreciate these two things about myself:

1. _____

2. _____

I am_____.

(POSITIVE AFFIRMATION)

Growing where you are planted. Even when people might say you can't do something... then just do it. They won't believe you can... until you do. Don't seek the approval of others to validate your desires and abilities. Believe you can, and you will. Be optimistic. Be relentless.

NeverStop.

I am grateful for these three things in my life

1. _____

2. _____

3. _____

I appreciate these two things about myself:

1. _____

2. _____

I am_____.

(POSITIVE AFFIRMATION)

If you ever start to think you have the world figured out, look for an opportunity to expand your vision of this amazing world and gain a broader perspective. Enjoy the vast amount of beauty that is right in front of our eyes.

NeverStop.

I am grateful for these three things in my life

1. _____

2. _____

3. _____

I appreciate these two things about myself:

1. _____

2. _____

I am_____.

(POSITIVE AFFIRMATION)

What we achieve may capture the eyes of others in the short term but who we are makes people remember us long after we are gone. Always be a good, kind hearted person because that will make a bigger impact on the world that accomplishing your goals.

NeverStop.

I am grateful for these three things in my life

1. _____

2. _____

3. _____

I appreciate these two things about myself:

1. _____

2. _____

I am_____.
　　　　　　　　　　(POSITIVE AFFIRMATION)

The choices we make today affect how we feel, think, and live tomorrow. Sometimes the answer is to just do the work instead of looking for an easy option. That easy option won't help you grow and it will likely take you longer to get to your goal.

NeverStop.

I am grateful for these three things in my life

1. _____

2. _____

3. _____

I appreciate these two things about myself:

1. _____

2. _____

I am_____.
(POSITIVE AFFIRMATION)

If you don't really know what you want, it is very difficult to get it. You will never accomplish a goal you never set. Be clear with your goals and be bold enough to put in the work and effort.

NeverStop.

I am grateful for these three things in my life

1. _____

2. _____

3. _____

I appreciate these two things about myself:

1. _____

2. _____

I am_____.
(POSITIVE AFFIRMATION)

The world is not against you. Once you truly believe that, things that don't go the way you planned will be moments of reflection, not frustration. Cultivate a steadfast belief that good things are coming and that everything in our life is divinely meant for us. Focus more on the good and you will lose sight of the bad.

NeverStop.

I am grateful for these three things in my life

    1. _____

    2. _____

    3. _____

I appreciate these two things about myself:

    1. _____

    2. _____

I am_____.
                                    (POSITIVE AFFIRMATION)

Don't make things worse that they really are. We can then tolerate the challenging things that come up in order to exist. Make the world a better place because we truly don't have anything else better to do. Be the bridge from where we are to where we could be and should be.

NeverStop.

I am grateful for these three things in my life

1. _____

2. _____

3. _____

I appreciate these two things about myself:

1. _____

2. _____

I am_____.
(POSITIVE AFFIRMATION)

Have the courage to take responsibility for yourself. The courage to resist the status quo and the desire to "fit in." Plus, we need to have the courage to stand up for what's right. When optimism and courage are present, hope still remains. Trust in your purpose and your ability to make a positive change in your life. Be bold, be kind, be courageous.

NeverStop.

I am grateful for these three things in my life

1. _____

2. _____

3. _____

I appreciate these two things about myself:

1. _____

2. _____

I am_____.

(POSITIVE AFFIRMATION)

Self-awareness is the starting point to a new mindset. Generate kindness, love, and happiness internally first so you can share it with others. It's tough to share what you don't have. Invest in yourself, find happiness in your life, not in things and spread your happiness.

NeverStop.

I am grateful for these three things in my life

1. _____

2. _____

3. _____

I appreciate these two things about myself:

1. _____

2. _____

I am_____.
(POSITIVE AFFIRMATION)

Our belief that we can accomplish something is a decision we have to make on our own. Our belief that we can is not based on our ability, it is based on your own level of investment in what we are trying to accomplish. If you believe you can, you will… because you are willing to do what it takes. Believe in yourself because of the strength inside of you.

NeverStop.

I am grateful for these three things in my life

1. _____

2. _____

3. _____

I appreciate these two things about myself:

1. _____

2. _____

I am_____.
                        (POSITIVE AFFIRMATION)

When you set goals, don't get caught up in needing the approval of others in order to believe you can achieve it. Your goals are meant for you, not them. Begin every goal with the end in mind. You are capable of doing great things. The world needs you to be who you are meant to be.

NeverStop.

I am grateful for these three things in my life

1. _____

2. _____

3. _____

I appreciate these two things about myself:

1. _____

2. _____

I am_____.
(POSITIVE AFFIRMATION)

Care for yourself in the same way that you treat someone you actually care deeply about. Practice self-love and surround yourself with things that you help grow in heart, mind and soul.

NeverStop.

I am grateful for these three things in my life

1. _____

2. _____

3. _____

I appreciate these two things about myself:

1. _____

2. _____

I am_____.

(POSITIVE AFFIRMATION)

Be alert to the beauty in life and especially the unexpected beauty in life. This tree isn't dying, its merely changing its leaves ahead of the other trees. Assume and judge less, appreciate more. Keep your head up and your perspective just might change.

NeverStop.

I am grateful for these three things in my life

1. _____

2. _____

3. _____

I appreciate these two things about myself:

1. _____

2. _____

I am_____.
(POSITIVE AFFIRMATION)

Don't live your life obsessed with satisfying everyone else. You won't be able to make everyone else happy. We each must decide on our own happiness. Just be you. Do the best you can and spread your goodness.

NeverStop.

I am grateful for these three things in my life

1. _____

2. _____

3. _____

I appreciate these two things about myself:

1. _____

2. _____

I am_____.
(POSITIVE AFFIRMATION)

We aren't going to live on this beautiful earth forever. We only get one shot at this amazing life. Each morning, be completely filled with gratitude that you have been blessed with another day. Decide to live each day in appreciation, in happiness, in hope, and in love.

NeverStop.

I am grateful for these three things in my life

1. _____

2. _____

3. _____

I appreciate these two things about myself:

1. _____

2. _____

I am_____.

(POSITIVE AFFIRMATION)

Learn the difference between simple and easy. You don't need to spend time thinking of five reasons why you should do something you really want to do... because you only need one reason. Don't over complicate life when you have a compelling reason and desire that inspired you to start in the first place.

NeverStop.

I am grateful for these three things in my life

1. _____

2. _____

3. _____

I appreciate these two things about myself:

1. _____

2. _____

I am_____.
(POSITIVE AFFIRMATION)

Let life fill you with hope and gratitude. Everything you wanted and everything you have ever needed may have been right in front of you the whole time. Open your eyes to see ow amazing life really is. The things that matter the most are things you cannot buy.

NeverStop.

I am grateful for these three things in my life

1. _____

2. _____

3. _____

I appreciate these two things about myself:

1. _____

2. _____

I am_____.

(POSITIVE AFFIRMATION)

Improvisation is a key to accomplishing your goals. No matter how great a plan is, we must always be ready to improvise. Keep your eye on the target, be flexible in strategy, choose positivity, and remain optimistic.

NeverStop.

I am grateful for these three things in my life

1. _____

2. _____

3. _____

I appreciate these two things about myself:

1. _____

2. _____

I am_____.
(POSITIVE AFFIRMATION)

Just be your true self. Let others see who you truly are and the right people will see the best in you. Trust the right people and they will help bring out the best in you. Be your best, not just like the rest.

NeverStop.

I am grateful for these three things in my life

1. _____

2. _____

3. _____

I appreciate these two things about myself:

1. _____

2. _____

I am_____.
(POSITIVE AFFIRMATION)

Cultivate the skill of quieting your mind. Learn to think your thoughts, not just the thoughts of others. Learn to tune out the noise of the world and regain control when we start overthinking. Be transformed by things that renew your heart and mind.

NeverStop.

I am grateful for these three things in my life

1. _____

2. _____

3. _____

I appreciate these two things about myself:

1. _____

2. _____

I am_____.
(POSITIVE AFFIRMATION)

Don't let something break you if it isn't what built you. Remember where you came from and use your unique background to be confident, not timid. Every moment of your life is preparing you for the next. Trust in the timing of life and tryst in your purpose. Be strong. Be patient. Be humble. Be optimistic.

NeverStop.

I am grateful for these three things in my life

    1. _____

    2. _____

    3. _____

I appreciate these two things about myself:

    1. _____

    2. _____

I am_____.

                           (POSITIVE AFFIRMATION)

Live your life day by day. Take nothing for granted and be present in each moment. We assemble our lives thought by thought and action by action. Do what has been presented for you to do and do it well Develop daily habits that encourage, inspire, and fulfill you.

NeverStop.

I am grateful for these three things in my life

1. _____

2. _____

3. _____

I appreciate these two things about myself:

1. _____

2. _____

I am_____.
(POSITIVE AFFIRMATION)

It takes a lifetime to become who you are meant to be. Just be patient. Don't be so focused on the outcome because you will miss the joy of becoming who the world needs you to be. Our life is a journey that is meant to be enjoyed, not rushed. Be grateful, be present, be optimistic.

NeverStop.

I am grateful for these three things in my life

1. _____

2. _____

3. _____

I appreciate these two things about myself:

1. _____

2. _____

I am_____.
(POSITIVE AFFIRMATION)

Each of us has a guiding light inside of us. We have the power to recognize the right direction and the right choice but our fate decides when and where it puts those things in front of us in order for our light to shine upon them so that we may see it. Keep your eyes open and trust in the timing of life.

NeverStop.

I am grateful for these three things in my life

1. _____

2. _____

3. _____

I appreciate these two things about myself:

1. _____

2. _____

I am_____.
(POSITIVE AFFIRMATION)

Learn to push yourself without being hard on yourself. Use self-love to propel you to become your best. Start where you are... not from where you used to be. Let your heart and mind be transformed. Each day is a new start and a new opportunity to fulfill our potential.

NeverStop.

I am grateful for these three things in my life

1. _____

2. _____

3. _____

I appreciate these two things about myself:

1. _____

2. _____

I am_____.

(POSITIVE AFFIRMATION)

We get to control our mindset no matter what. To me, optimism isn't about how much water I see in a glass. I am just grateful I have a glass and I am always optimistic that it can be filled up with fulfilling moments in my life. We are only a decision away from seeing the world with a new perspective.

NeverStop.

I am grateful for these three things in my life

1. _____

2. _____

3. _____

I appreciate these two things about myself:

1. _____

2. _____

I am_____.

(POSITIVE AFFIRMATION)

Never let your expectations of something ruin your experience. It's great to look forward to things but learn to be present in each moment. Appreciate something for what it is, not what you thought it was going to be. Live in each moment that has always been meant for you.

NeverStop.

I am grateful for these three things in my life

1. _____

2. _____

3. _____

I appreciate these two things about myself:

1. _____

2. _____

I am_____.

(POSITIVE AFFIRMATION)

Never be ashamed of your story. You were meant to be different, not the same. Learn to love your difference because that is what makes the world so beautiful. No matter where you are on your journey, you are always enough.

NeverStop.

I am grateful for these three things in my life

1. _____

2. _____

3. _____

I appreciate these two things about myself:

1. _____

2. _____

I am_____.
(POSITIVE AFFIRMATION)

We may not always get what we want but we must maintain a grateful heart. Constantly be aware of how great your life really is, not just how it may feel moment to moment. Look for gifts of love and let it give you hope and optimism.

NeverStop.

I am grateful for these three things in my life

1. _____

2. _____

3. _____

I appreciate these two things about myself:

1. _____

2. _____

I am_____.

(POSITIVE AFFIRMATION)

Practice daily habits that enhance your strengths and help you get closer to where you want to be. What we do every day will reflect what we want to become. Use your passion to strengthen your daily habits. Pursue your purpose with relentless hope and optimism.

NeverStop.

I am grateful for these three things in my life

    1. _____

    2. _____

    3. _____

I appreciate these two things about myself:

    1. _____

    2. _____

I am_____.
                        (POSITIVE AFFIRMATION)

Stay in control of your mind. Realize that anger only happens when we lose control of our thoughts and typically when we are paying too much attention to something. No one can offend you without your permission. Choose your thoughts, choose your mindset, and choose to see all of beauty in life. Be quick to listen and love.

NeverStop.

I am grateful for these three things in my life

1. _____

2. _____

3. _____

I appreciate these two things about myself:

1. _____

2. _____

I am_____.
(POSITIVE AFFIRMATION)

We must take action in our lives. Talking is not taking action. What we do reflects who we are and reflects our choices. Who we are shows up in how we live and how we treat others. Be kind. Be humble.

NeverStop.

I am grateful for these three things in my life

1. _____

2. _____

3. _____

I appreciate these two things about myself:

1. _____

2. _____

I am_____.
(POSITIVE AFFIRMATION)

Teach yourself to worry less. If it's in your control, then you need to put the work in. if it's out of your control, then trust in fate and the perfect timing of life. In either case, there are only two options: Make the most of the good times. Make the most of the bad times.

NeverStop.

I am grateful for these three things in my life

    1. _____

    2. _____

    3. _____

I appreciate these two things about myself:

    1. _____

    2. _____

I am_____.

                        (POSITIVE AFFIRMATION)

Be a good person and never take more than you need. Be aware of the needs of others. Since there are so many good people in the world, you have a chance to get something for yourself in the first place. Choose love.

NeverStop.

I am grateful for these three things in my life

1. _____

2. _____

3. _____

I appreciate these two things about myself:

1. _____

2. _____

I am_____.
(POSITIVE AFFIRMATION)

Spend less time worrying about temporary things. Instead, focus on the everlasting steadfast things in your life. In the moment, temporary things can seem like everything but we must realize it is just momentary and the steadfast things in our life will be there when it's gone.

NeverStop.

I am grateful for these three things in my life

1. _____

2. _____

3. _____

I appreciate these two things about myself:

1. _____

2. _____

I am_____.

(POSITIVE AFFIRMATION)

Whatever is true, whatever is honorable, whatever is just, whatever is pure, whatever is lovely, whatever is commendable, if there is any excellence, if there is anything worthy of praise, think about these things. Choose your mindset..

NeverStop.

I am grateful for these three things in my life

1. _____

2. _____

3. _____

I appreciate these two things about myself:

1. _____

2. _____

I am_____.

(POSITIVE AFFIRMATION)

Even in the midst of noise, distraction, negativity, or troubles in life...Be calm in your heart and be peaceful. Choose love. Have faith. Be an example.

NeverStop.

I am grateful for these three things in my life

1. _____

2. _____

3. _____

I appreciate these two things about myself:

1. _____

2. _____

I am_____.
(POSITIVE AFFIRMATION)

Kindness is more important than wisdom. Recognizing that is a sign of wisdom. Kindness is contagious. Be good to others to inspire others to be good to others. Choose love. Smile often.

NeverStop.

I am grateful for these three things in my life

    1. _____

    2. _____

    3. _____

I appreciate these two things about myself:

    1. _____

    2. _____

I am_____.

                        (POSITIVE AFFIRMATION)

Avoid living in the past and comparing yourself to others. Find happiness in who you are in each divine moment of your life. Invest in your mind, body, and soul and enjoy your unique journey.

NeverStop.

I am grateful for these three things in my life

    1. _____

    2. _____

    3. _____

I appreciate these two things about myself:

    1. _____

    2. _____

I am_____.
                             (POSITIVE AFFIRMATION)

Set goals you want to accomplish over the next year. You must also develop strategies. Share those with the people that are close to you so they can encourage you and be mindful of your goals. Cultivate unwavering belief in yourself because you know you are willing to put in the work and be patient while you make your progress.

NeverStop.

I am grateful for these three things in my life

1. _____

2. _____

3. _____

I appreciate these two things about myself:

1. _____

2. _____

I am_____.
(POSITIVE AFFIRMATION)

Be committed to working on yourself in preparation for where you want to be. Work on yourself before you work with others. Always know we can learn from everyone and others will learn from us. Be aware of what you are teaching those around you. Prepare your heart and mind and your actions will follow. Be patient with yourself. Focus more on why, not when.
Control what we can and let go of everything else.

NeverStop.

I am grateful for these three things in my life

1. _____

2. _____

3. _____

I appreciate these two things about myself:

1. _____

2. _____

I am_____.
(POSITIVE AFFIRMATION)

It's not just what we say and do that matters. It's much more about how we say what's on our hearts and how we treat others. Our spirit and heart behind what we do matters more than just the action. Be kind, be caring, be loving... not out of obligation but out of opportunity.

NeverStop.

I am grateful for these three things in my life

1. _____

2. _____

3. _____

I appreciate these two things about myself:

1. _____

2. _____

I am_____.

(POSITIVE AFFIRMATION)

There are times we cannot change circumstances in our life, but we can always change how we look at our circumstances. Instead of being frustrated, be fascinated. When you stop and think, the events in our lives are pretty incredible. Life is for us, not against us. If one thing doesn't go your way, focus more on the many things that are going your way. We will see more of what we focus on.

NeverStop.

I am grateful for these three things in my life

1. _____

2. _____

3. _____

I appreciate these two things about myself:

1. _____

2. _____

I am_____.

(POSITIVE AFFIRMATION)

No matter how long we have been doing something, it's always good to find perspective. Evaluate your habits to determine what is best, what is fair, and what is right. We need to find a balance with these especially since these may change with time. None of us have it all figured out so be patient with yourself.

NeverStop.

I am grateful for these three things in my life

1. _____

2. _____

3. _____

I appreciate these two things about myself:

1. _____

2. _____

I am_____.
(POSITIVE AFFIRMATION)

If are working towards a goal, don't just focus on the end result. If you do, it's easy to be frustrated or disheartened with yourself because you aren't where you want to be. Focus on the process, your level of daily commitment, and trust that hard work pays off. What it looks like at the end is unknown to us anyway. Have faith.

NeverStop.

I am grateful for these three things in my life

1. _____

2. _____

3. _____

I appreciate these two things about myself:

1. _____

2. _____

I am_____.

(POSITIVE AFFIRMATION)

We all need to choose what impact we want to have on others. Be an encourager. Be that person that recognizes other people's gifts and encourages them to use them. If someone tells you they want to accomplish something, encourage them with feedback in the name of love. Help others succeed as much as possible. We can't see the future so we might as well be optimistic.

NeverStop.

I am grateful for these three things in my life

1. _____

2. _____

3. _____

I appreciate these two things about myself:

1. _____

2. _____

I am_____.
(POSITIVE AFFIRMATION)

We don't need to know the answers to everything in life. Some things should just be enjoyed for what they are. Don't get caught up in trying to figure something out that is not meant to be figured out. Be present and have a quiet mind while feeling grateful. Experience life to the fullest. We don't know what tomorrow will bring so don't concern yourself with what will happen a year from now.

NeverStop.

I am grateful for these three things in my life

1. _____

2. _____

3. _____

I appreciate these two things about myself:

1. _____

2. _____

I am_____.
(POSITIVE AFFIRMATION)

Your list of goals and things you're grateful for should always be longer than a list of things you think aren't going well in your life. It is important to keep both lists because the things that you wish were different provides great insight as to what you would be passionate about working on. Which list you focus on is up to you. Choose gratitude, humility, and kindness.

NeverStop.

I am grateful for these three things in my life

    1. _____

    2. _____

    3. _____

I appreciate these two things about myself:

    1. _____

    2. _____

I am_____.

                            (POSITIVE AFFIRMATION)

The importance of your self-image is much more important than how others see you. See your value from the inside out. What others see on the outside is a direct reflection of what we see in ourselves on the inside. Shine your light regardless of what other people see or what light they shine. Your light is unique to you. Individually, it is beautiful...but together, our light is breathtaking. Treat your mind and body with love, not regret and hate. Love must come from within first.

NeverStop.

I am grateful for these three things in my life

1. _____

2. _____

3. _____

I appreciate these two things about myself:

1. _____

2. _____

I am_____.

(POSITIVE AFFIRMATION)

The more you take, the less you have. Need what you have, not what you want. Clutter and excess distracts us because we cannot see all that we have. Give more to others and you will receive more. We can give away energy, time, effort, love, kindness every day. We have something special to give back that can make the world a better place. Give from your heart.

NeverStop.

I am grateful for these three things in my life

1. _____

2. _____

3. _____

I appreciate these two things about myself:

1. _____

2. _____

I am_____.

(POSITIVE AFFIRMATION)

Our time is short but feels long. Our days are numbered but it's paramount to not count them. We never know how many we have besides the day we have been blessed with today. What was, what is, what will be...we can only be present in one of those places. Be aware of where you spend your time. Trust in the bigger plan. Love each day with a grateful, loving heart.

NeverStop.

I am grateful for these three things in my life

1. _____

2. _____

3. _____

I appreciate these two things about myself:

1. _____

2. _____

I am_____.
(POSITIVE AFFIRMATION)

Don't get caught up in feeling like you have to wait until you are completely ready to start pursuing something. No one is ever totally ready and we don't get to choose our time. We can only prepare ourselves and recognize the opportunities we are blessed with. The sun will shine the next morning whether we are ready for it or not. Trust in your gifts and your ability to work hard in order to feel ready to pursue what is on your heart.

NeverStop.

I am grateful for these three things in my life

1. _____

2. _____

3. _____

I appreciate these two things about myself:

1. _____

2. _____

I am_____.
(POSITIVE AFFIRMATION)

If there is something you want to do but feel scared, once you take the first step...your fear will begin to subside. Our fear is often our lack of belief in our ability to do that very thing, not the thing itself. See fear as enhanced thoughtfulness and awareness, not an inability to do something. Trust that you have more in you that you haven't discovered yet. Challenges are opportunities to see the strength within us.

NeverStop.

I am grateful for these three things in my life

1. _____

2. _____

3. _____

I appreciate these two things about myself:

1. _____

2. _____

I am_____.

(POSITIVE AFFIRMATION)

We learn lessons in life because we are loved. Sometimes we learn that the thing we've been searching for our whole lives has been right next to us all along. We just weren't ready to see the value of it when it first came in to our life. Always know that you are enough, you are capable, and you are significant. You are here on purpose, not by chance.

NeverStop.

I am grateful for these three things in my life

1. _____

2. _____

3. _____

I appreciate these two things about myself:

1. _____

2. _____

I am_____.
(POSITIVE AFFIRMATION)

Be full of so much goodness on the inside that you don't have to worry about looking like you are good on the outside. People will see kindness, gratitude, and love by seeing how you treat others. What's inside of us always gets squeezed out of us. Spend just as much time working on your heart and mind as you do trying to improve your body. Positivity and goodness always wins.

NeverStop.

I am grateful for these three things in my life

1. _____

2. _____

3. _____

I appreciate these two things about myself:

1. _____

2. _____

I am_____.

(POSITIVE AFFIRMATION)

Never let a day go by without thinking about what you're grateful for. Some of the simple things like waking up in the morning, having a bed to sleep on, having clothes to wear, having a job, having a car to get to that job, are all things that we should never take for granted. Just the fact that you can log into Social media means that your life is pretty good. Be humble. Cultivate an attitude of gratitude.

NeverStop.

I am grateful for these three things in my life

1. _____

2. _____

3. _____

I appreciate these two things about myself:

1. _____

2. _____

I am_____.

(POSITIVE AFFIRMATION)

Just because something didn't turn out the way you expected, trust that it could turn out to be even better than what you had planned. Always be hopeful that great things are coming in your life. Keep your head up so that you will see the blessings coming. Trust in the timing of life. You will receive all that you need when you are ready for it. Be optimistic, be hopeful, have faith.

NeverStop.

I am grateful for these three things in my life

1. _____

2. _____

3. _____

I appreciate these two things about myself:

1. _____

2. _____

I am_____.

(POSITIVE AFFIRMATION)

We often set goals only as far as we can see. However, when we get there, we can still see beyond that point. Don't limit yourself based on eyesight, push yourself with a vision. We are all capable of doing amazing things when we are willing to believe in the strength we have inside of us. Time will reveal that we have always been all that we needed to be.

NeverStop.

I am grateful for these three things in my life

1. _____

2. _____

3. _____

I appreciate these two things about myself:

1. _____

2. _____

I am_____.

(POSITIVE AFFIRMATION)

Never let a tough day affect your next day. It is so important to let things go so you can see how good life is. Don't let a bad moment turn in to a bad day or bad week or a bad year. Finish each day with a moment of acceptance, gratitude, and faith. Be grateful for the start of a new day and make each day a great day. We will find what we are looking for so look for the blessings.

NeverStop.

I am grateful for these three things in my life

1. _____

2. _____

3. _____

I appreciate these two things about myself:

1. _____

2. _____

I am_____.

(POSITIVE AFFIRMATION)

Humility is a matter of the mind and the heart. Be humble enough to know that you aren't better than anyone else while being wise enough to realize that you are different than others. When we are humbled by events, our hearts become transformed. What's in our hearts will determine how we think, speak, and act. Never boast or make excuses, we are all on our own journey.

NeverStop.

I am grateful for these three things in my life

1. _____

2. _____

3. _____

I appreciate these two things about myself:

1. _____

2. _____

I am_____.
(POSITIVE AFFIRMATION)

Don't get caught up in looking for the easy way out or the easy solution. What comes easy goes easy. Do the things that are difficult because that will lead to growth and will make it hard to take it away from you. With challenges comes opportunities to fulfill your potential. You are much stronger than you realize. The strength inside of you is all you need.

NeverStop.

I am grateful for these three things in my life

1. _____

2. _____

3. _____

I appreciate these two things about myself:

1. _____

2. _____

I am_____.
(POSITIVE AFFIRMATION)

The first step to changing anything is knowing and accepting that we have chosen it to be what it is. That allows us to see that if we choose for it to change, it can be changed. Change starts with self-awareness and self-reflection. It's never too late to start new habits. Change at your pace and don't get stressed if others change faster. Direction is more important than speed.

NeverStop.

I am grateful for these three things in my life

1. _____

2. _____

3. _____

I appreciate these two things about myself:

1. _____

2. _____

I am_____.

(POSITIVE AFFIRMATION)

Cultivate the skill of being patient. Being patient is a decision and is a form of taking action. Waiting is passive, being vpatient is being active. When something doesn't work out when you expected it to, that is an opportunity to cultivate patience. Be patient after putting in the work and believe that the work will pay off. The timing of life is always perfect. Optimism and faith is key while being patient.

NeverStop.

I am grateful for these three things in my life

1. _____

2. _____

3. _____

I appreciate these two things about myself:

1. _____

2. _____

I am_____.
(POSITIVE AFFIRMATION)

Who we are on the inside determines what we see on the outside. We may look at the same thing but not see the same thing. We always have control of what's inside of us. See opportunity when others see obligations. See blessings when others see burden. Cultivate a mindset of gratitude and you will see the world differently.

NeverStop.

I am grateful for these three things in my life

1. _____

2. _____

3. _____

I appreciate these two things about myself:

1. _____

2. _____

I am_____.
(POSITIVE AFFIRMATION)

Worrying about the future doesn't benefit us. In fact, it makes each day heavier than it needs to be. Don't carry that burden because it just takes our daily strength more than it relieves any worry. Believe that you can and it's already done. Trust in the bigger plan and use your gifts.
You are strong, able, and significant.

NeverStop.

I am grateful for these three things in my life

1. _____

2. _____

3. _____

I appreciate these two things about myself:

1. _____

2. _____

I am_____.

(POSITIVE AFFIRMATION)

Never let anything take away your joy and your spirit. We are never too old to enjoy life and to be excited about things. Happiness and excitement is contiguous. Never lose your playful spirit. Your joy could make others smile. What makes us excited may change but that we get excited is our choice. Look forward to life more than you wait for it..

NeverStop.

I am grateful for these three things in my life

1. _____

2. _____

3. _____

I appreciate these two things about myself:

1. _____

2. _____

I am_____.
(POSITIVE AFFIRMATION)

Learn to cultivate an unwavering belief in yourself. Not out of arrogance but out of trust and faith. We can't name a situation that we haven't made it through so far in our lives. Learn from your past. Your talents and abilities may seem unknown but in fact they are just temporarily hidden and waiting to be realized. Trust in yourself because you.

NeverStop.

I am grateful for these three things in my life

1. _____
2. _____
3. _____

I appreciate these two things about myself:

1. _____
2. _____

I am_____.
(POSITIVE AFFIRMATION)

If you want to cultivate a new mindset, it will take daily discipline. It will be very hard to find and adopt a new mindset if we never let go of our old one. Focus more on why your mindset changed, not just how. Our sense of purpose is true in all areas of our lives. Always know you have the ability to control your own thoughts, words, and actions. It's a blessing that we often take for granted.

NeverStop.

I am grateful for these three things in my life

1. _____

2. _____

3. _____

I appreciate these two things about myself:

1. _____

2. _____

I am_____.

(POSITIVE AFFIRMATION)

When you are pursuing change in your life, there might be people trying to help you stay the same. It's important to write down your goals for yourself and be specific. Don't let it affect you when others question your ability...they don't know the kind of work you are willing to do. Be made new, don't just try new things. Commit to the new strategy and lose the old strategy of comfort. Trust in yourself because of the strength inside of you..

NeverStop.

I am grateful for these three things in my life

1. _____

2. _____

3. _____

I appreciate these two things about myself:

1. _____

2. _____

I am_____.
(POSITIVE AFFIRMATION)

One thing the world needs more of is love. Be so full of love that you don't have room for any negativity. Leave no room for greed, jealousy or anger. Sound, look, and act like love. Be patient, be kind, never boast, never count wrong doings, don't be angered, and find peace in truth. Always trust, always have hope, always persevere. Choose love, it always wins.

NeverStop.

I am grateful for these three things in my life

    1. _____

    2. _____

    3. _____

I appreciate these two things about myself:

    1. _____

    2. _____

I am_____.

                        (POSITIVE AFFIRMATION)

It's important to learn from mistakes. We can either make the mistake ourselves or learn from others. We will keep making the same mistake until we learn the lesson it is meant to teach us. Life isn't about not making mistakes, it's always about learning from them. Mistakes are effort in action. Appreciate effort more than just the outcome. Be patient. Be humble.

NeverStop.

I am grateful for these three things in my life

1. _____

2. _____

3. _____

I appreciate these two things about myself:

1. _____

2. _____

I am_____.

(POSITIVE AFFIRMATION)

We are a lot more similar than we are different. Our similarities should be bring us to together more than our differences pull us apart. We all have the same basic core needs. However, how we pursue those needs looks different for others. We were all created with gifts but it's up to us to use those gifts to make a positive difference. You are enough.

NeverStop.

I am grateful for these three things in my life

    1. _____

    2. _____

    3. _____

I appreciate these two things about myself:

    1. _____

    2. _____

I am_____.
                           (POSITIVE AFFIRMATION)

There are times we need to do things that we don't necessarily want to do. However, there is a very meaningful reason why we are being asked to do it. Focus less on what the task is and more on why the task needs to be done. It may be an opportunity to use your gifts. Live life on purpose, for a purpose.

NeverStop.

I am grateful for these three things in my life

1. _____

2. _____

3. _____

I appreciate these two things about myself:

1. _____

2. _____

I am_____.
                            (POSITIVE AFFIRMATION)

We can't just hope things get better if we aren't willing to improve ourselves. Motivate yourself before you expect to motivate others. Lead by example and model the right behaviors. Be the change while understanding that others will change at their own pace. True change comes from the inside. We all know better so encourage each other to do better.

NeverStop.

I am grateful for these three things in my life

1. _____

2. _____

3. _____

I appreciate these two things about myself:

1. _____

2. _____

I am_____.
(POSITIVE AFFIRMATION)

When we only focus on improving our body, we lose our minds. Get your head right and your body will feel great. We need to prepare our minds before we prepare our body. Our mind affects the heart and the heart affects the body. Every meal matters, every conversation matters, everything we read matters... Great things take time. Everything will happen right when it is supposed to.

NeverStop.

I am grateful for these three things in my life

1. _____

2. _____

3. _____

I appreciate these two things about myself:

1. _____

2. _____

I am_____.
      (POSITIVE AFFIRMATION)

Don't get caught up in the value of things just because they are new. Some of the most valuable things we have are things we have had all along. Expensive doesn't always mean valuable. If you aren't happy with what you have now, you won't be happy with more. Give back more than you receive.

NeverStop.

I am grateful for these three things in my life

1. _____

2. _____

3. _____

I appreciate these two things about myself:

1. _____

2. _____

I am_____.
(POSITIVE AFFIRMATION)

What we set our minds on dictates our direction. Focus more on what you want, not what you don't want. If you want to see more of something, just focus on it. Typically, we will find what we are looking for. Be in control of your mindset and thoughts. Never let the environment dictate your desires. The energy we bring affects our environment. Be kind. Be grateful.

NeverStop.

I am grateful for these three things in my life

1. _____

2. _____

3. _____

I appreciate these two things about myself:

1. _____

2. _____

I am_____.

(POSITIVE AFFIRMATION)

Your talents are worth developing and caring for. We were created with unique gifts. The world needs you to be you, not anyone else. Follow your heart and contribute what you can because the world needs you to. We only get so much time in life, so cherish every second. Develop your talents, be humble, and inspire others.

NeverStop.

I am grateful for these three things in my life

1. _____

2. _____

3. _____

I appreciate these two things about myself:

1. _____

2. _____

I am_____.

(POSITIVE AFFIRMATION)

Some of the things that we never saw coming end up being exactly the things we needed to see. Life is not meant to be figured out, it should be lived and enjoyed. Make the most out of every opportunity we are blessed with. Do more than what is expected when others least expect it.

NeverStop.

I am grateful for these three things in my life

1. _____

2. _____

3. _____

I appreciate these two things about myself:

1. _____

2. _____

I am_____.
(POSITIVE AFFIRMATION)

Running away from our problems may be easier but always remember it is only a temporary solution. Face the problems we are presented with a soft heart and open mind. Our future should never be limited because of our past. Don't procrastinate your life away. Take responsibility to change situations that don't light the fire in your soul. Take action in life.

NeverStop.

I am grateful for these three things in my life

1. _____

2. _____

3. _____

I appreciate these two things about myself:

1. _____

2. _____

I am_____.

(POSITIVE AFFIRMATION)

People will show you who they really are. You should believe them. Always remember your effort and actions matter. They show people how we think of them. Use words to affirm your actions, not contradict them. Show more love to express more love. In the best times and worst times, people will always remember how we made them feel. Be kind.

NeverStop.

I am grateful for these three things in my life

1. _____

2. _____

3. _____

I appreciate these two things about myself:

1. _____

2. _____

I am_____.

(POSITIVE AFFIRMATION)

The words we use matter to the minds and hearts of those we are lucky enough to have in our lives. We can't be positive and negative at the same time so be positive. Look for the great things about people instead of looking for flaws. See others as we would want to be seen.
Compliment more than you criticize. Never blow out someone else's light to make your light shine brighter. Together we are a brighter light. Kindness and positivity always wins.

NeverStop.

I am grateful for these three things in my life

1. _____

2. _____

3. _____

I appreciate these two things about myself:

1. _____

2. _____

I am_____.
(POSITIVE AFFIRMATION)

Let go of the past if it is weighing you down. Learn from it. You are not the same person that you were back then. Each day we are given the blessing to start each day and to be made new. If you want change, do it now. If you know how to change, make the decision and commitment that you will and you must. Love yourself enough to take care of yourself. Believe in yourself because of what you are.

NeverStop.

I am grateful for these three things in my life

1. _____

2. _____

3. _____

I appreciate these two things about myself:

1. _____

2. _____

I am_____.
(POSITIVE AFFIRMATION)

A clear conscience is a result of clear thinking or troubled thinking that doesn't affect us anymore. Spend time clearing your mind of things that are heavy. Let go out what we cannot control, control what we can, and find the wisdom to know the difference. Love to live and live to love.

NeverStop.

I am grateful for these three things in my life

1. _____

2. _____

3. _____

I appreciate these two things about myself:

1. _____

2. _____

I am_____.
                    (POSITIVE AFFIRMATION)

We have a lot to offer to those around us. One of the most important things is our time. We show value in others by giving time to listen, to talk, or help with anything. Spend more time serving than you do being served. Always make time for others.

NeverStop.

I am grateful for these three things in my life

    1. _____

    2. _____

    3. _____

I appreciate these two things about myself:

    1. _____

    2. _____

I am_____.

                          (POSITIVE AFFIRMATION)

Cultivate belief in yourself and a constant sense of optimism. Believe that you can use your gifts to find a way to overcome any obstacles or accomplish any goals you have. No matter what, no matter how long it takes, always find a way. The process of finding a way reveals our potential. Believe you can and it's already done.

NeverStop.

I am grateful for these three things in my life

1. _____

2. _____

3. _____

I appreciate these two things about myself:

1. _____

2. _____

I am_____.
(POSITIVE AFFIRMATION)

Focus more on becoming more resourceful instead of always feeling like you need more resources. Sometimes too many resources distracts us and prevents us from fulfilling our potential. Having too many things can keep us from seeing that we have all that we need. Be grateful for what you have and use the gifts you have been given. Be patient. Be optimistic.

NeverStop.

I am grateful for these three things in my life

1. _____

2. _____

3. _____

I appreciate these two things about myself:

1. _____

2. _____

I am_____.

(POSITIVE AFFIRMATION)

Develop habits that help you do what you say you are going to do. Plan the night before, write a to-do list, keep notes on your phone, make morning or evening goals, etc...Doing what we say we are going to do matters to others and it makes us feel good. Make a list and check it off.

When you don't get to everything on the list (or you forget), don't make excuses, be humbled and commit to doing better. The follow through always matters.

NeverStop.

I am grateful for these three things in my life

1. _____

2. _____

3. _____

I appreciate these two things about myself:

1. _____

2. _____

I am_____.
(POSITIVE AFFIRMATION)

Always be aware of how your words and actions impact others. Never have the goal of having a big impact if it negatively affects those around you. When having an impact, change may happen, but be mindful and strive to cultivate positive change. We should never push others down in order for us to accomplish our goals. Have others in mind. Soften your heart.

NeverStop.

I am grateful for these three things in my life

1. _____

2. _____

3. _____

I appreciate these two things about myself:

1. _____

2. _____

I am_____.
(POSITIVE AFFIRMATION)

Never take a goodbye for granted. Make sure your goodbyes are mindful and purposeful. We never know how many days we have so be grateful for every moment. Say goodbye in a way that makes people feel like you already can't wait to see them again. Make them happier that they got to see you than sad because they had to leave you. People remember how we make them feel. Be kind. Choose love.

NeverStop.

I am grateful for these three things in my life

    1. _____

    2. _____

    3. _____

I appreciate these two things about myself:

    1. _____

    2. _____

I am_____.
                            (POSITIVE AFFIRMATION)

Effort always matters. Anticipate the needs of others to show them that you care. Open a door, make dinner, reach out a hand, wish them good luck, let people over in traffic, surprise people with their favorite something, etc... When you show people you want to help even before they ask, it means a lot. It shows that you think of them more often than they think. Serving others looks like love.

NeverStop.

I am grateful for these three things in my life

1. _____

2. _____

3. _____

I appreciate these two things about myself:

1. _____

2. _____

I am_____.
(POSITIVE AFFIRMATION)

The way we greet people says a lot about how we think of them. We have the ability to make others feel valuable just by greeting them with a warm heart and open arms. You never know when a smile can brighten someone's day. Smile more, it's contagious. Be the first one to smile and see what happens. Greet others how you want to be greeted. Every moments matters.
Love to live life.

NeverStop.

I am grateful for these three things in my life

1. _____

2. _____

3. _____

I appreciate these two things about myself:

1. _____

2. _____

I am_____.
(POSITIVE AFFIRMATION)

Effort always matters. Anticipate the needs of others to show them that you care. Open a door, make dinner, reach out a hand, wish them good luck, let people over in traffic, surprise people with their favorite something, etc... When you show people you want to help even before they ask, it means a lot. It shows that you think of them more often than they think. Serving others looks like love.

NeverStop.

I am grateful for these three things in my life

1. _____

2. _____

3. _____

I appreciate these two things about myself:

1. _____

2. _____

I am_____.

(POSITIVE AFFIRMATION)

Make sure to be mindful with social media. When you are around other people, be present with those people. When you are in public, you never know when having your head up and acknowledging others might lead to a great opportunity. Use social media, don't let it use you. Life is short, don't let it pass you by with your head down. Don't miss the beauty in life.

NeverStop.

I am grateful for these three things in my life

1. _____

2. _____

3. _____

I appreciate these two things about myself:

1. _____

2. _____

I am_____.

(POSITIVE AFFIRMATION)

The things that go left unsaid can often do the most damage. Plus, the things we never say, always stay with us. Share your words with a mindful heart. Be honest and kind. Open yourself up and ask for others to give you feedback on how to improve. Cultivate relationships strong in trust and communication. Offer each other moments of grace.

NeverStop.

I am grateful for these three things in my life

1. _____

2. _____

3. _____

I appreciate these two things about myself:

1. _____

2. _____

I am_____.
(POSITIVE AFFIRMATION)

Give more energy to you dreams and goals than you do your fears. Where our energy goes, our thoughts will follow. Focus more on what could go right and less on what could go wrong. Be in control of your own mindset and surround yourself with people that encourage you. Believe in yourself because you believe in the bigger plan.

NeverStop.

I am grateful for these three things in my life

1. _____

2. _____

3. _____

I appreciate these two things about myself:

1. _____

2. _____

I am_____.
(POSITIVE AFFIRMATION)

Don't get too caught up in the desire to fit in. We are all different so just be your true self. No two minds are the same, no two hearts are the same, no two bodies are the same. You are way too unique and valuable to try to be the same as everyone else. Love, respect, and learn from our differences and don't judge people by them.

NeverStop.

I am grateful for these three things in my life

1. _____

2. _____

3. _____

I appreciate these two things about myself:

1. _____

2. _____

I am_____.

(POSITIVE AFFIRMATION)

Pay attention to what we are pushed and pulled to do. We are pushed externally and pulled internally. The things we are pushed to do can be out of obligation or a desire to change. The things we are pulled to do are out of opportunity and the desire to be changed. Being pulled to do something often feels like it is bigger than ourselves. The push and pull are positive and we need both.

NeverStop.

I am grateful for these three things in my life

1. _____

2. _____

3. _____

I appreciate these two things about myself:

1. _____

2. _____

I am_____.
(POSITIVE AFFIRMATION)

There will be accidents that happen in life but there is nothing accidental about your life. Every single one of us is able to make the world a better place and we have a unique purpose. Never underestimate your value or ability to influence those around us. Think about your purpose for min first thing in the morning and set your focus for the day. Be humble. Be grateful.

NeverStop.

I am grateful for these three things in my life

1. _____

2. _____

3. _____

I appreciate these two things about myself:

1. _____

2. _____

I am_____.
(POSITIVE AFFIRMATION)

Set goals that transform your heart and mind while you are working to accomplish them. The accomplishment of the goal is inspiring but the amazing thing to realize is how we have been transformed while we were working on it. Cultivate a deeper sense of self-belief to set higher goals.

NeverStop.

I am grateful for these three things in my life

1. _____

2. _____

3. _____

I appreciate these two things about myself:

1. _____

2. _____

I am_____.
(POSITIVE AFFIRMATION)

If we want things to change, we also have to be willing to change. If we want things to better, we must commit to being and doing better. If we want others to do the right thing, we should first start by doing the right thing ourselves. You never know who is watching you or relying on you to be an example. That is an opportunity to influence, not pressure to be perfect. Be purposeful with your actions.

NeverStop.

I am grateful for these three things in my life

1. _____

2. _____

3. _____

I appreciate these two things about myself:

1. _____

2. _____

I am_____.

(POSITIVE AFFIRMATION)

Time is much more valuable than money. We can get more money but we cannot get more time. How we spend our time is more important than how we spend our money. We will always wish we had more time...only sometimes wish we had more money. See the value of just spending time doings things you love with people you love. People care about more time with you than what you bought anyway. Be present in the moment.

NeverStop.

I am grateful for these three things in my life

1. _____

2. _____

3. _____

I appreciate these two things about myself:

1. _____

2. _____

I am_____.
(POSITIVE AFFIRMATION)

Spend more time thinking about, and discussing, how good life is and how great it can still become. Then, make a plan and development strategies to constantly remind yourself of your vision and plan. Spend less time complaining about how things used to be. Those days are history. Be optimistic. Be hopeful. Be humble.

NeverStop.

I am grateful for these three things in my life

1. _____

2. _____

3. _____

I appreciate these two things about myself:

1. _____

2. _____

I am_____.
(POSITIVE AFFIRMATION)

Take action because you love, not because you hate. If you want to lose weight, put in the effort because you love your body, not because you hate it. If you want a new job, get a job you love as opposed to just leaving a job you hate. Do what you do with the thought of what is to come, not to avoid what was. Keep your focus forward. Choose your mindset.

NeverStop.

I am grateful for these three things in my life

1. _____

2. _____

3. _____

I appreciate these two things about myself:

1. _____

2. _____

I am_____.
(POSITIVE AFFIRMATION)

Be a student in life. Learn from books, from people, and your own experiences. If you are needing to go to school or read a book to enhance your skills, see that learning as the path to your success, not the barrier. Knowledge allows us to help others and ourselves. Seek wisdom and believe in yourself.

NeverStop.

I am grateful for these three things in my life

1. _____

2. _____

3. _____

I appreciate these two things about myself:

1. _____

2. _____

I am_____.

(POSITIVE AFFIRMATION)

We are attracted to people in our lives that look like or sound like how we see ourselves. Surround yourself with people that help you and encourage you to grow. Life is too short to be surrounded by negativity, selfishness, pessimism and judgement. Live life to fulfill your potential, not meet the minimums. We have been created to do great things. We are in control of who we spend our time with. Never judge anyone. Be encouraged.

NeverStop.

I am grateful for these three things in my life

1. _____

2. _____

3. _____

I appreciate these two things about myself:

1. _____

2. _____

I am_____.

(POSITIVE AFFIRMATION)

Great things happen when you don't give up even when you really want to. The world tends to reward the hearts and minds that are persistent and determined. That moment when you don't know if you can continue is often very close to the turning point you are hoping for. Believe in the great things to come and believe in your ability to withstand challenges.

NeverStop.

I am grateful for these three things in my life

1. _____

2. _____

3. _____

I appreciate these two things about myself:

1. _____

2. _____

I am_____.
(POSITIVE AFFIRMATION)

Comparing yourself to others will often steal our sense of joy, progress, and accomplishment. Plus, it will rarely lead to cultivating a growth mindset. Everyone is on their own journey made specifically for them. Encourage and inspire each other instead of trying to be better than others. Be the best you. You are strong, capable, and significant.

NeverStop.

I am grateful for these three things in my life

1. _____

2. _____

3. _____

I appreciate these two things about myself:

1. _____

2. _____

I am_____.

(POSITIVE AFFIRMATION)

Never take a day for granted. Never take other people and their effort to be in your life for granted. Be present in every moment to feel more appreciation than anxiety. Recognize the joy that people bring to your life and make time to thank them. We should never be too busy to be a good, caring, appreciative person. Be humble.

NeverStop.

I am grateful for these three things in my life

1. _____

2. _____

3. _____

I appreciate these two things about myself:

1. _____

2. _____

I am_____.
(POSITIVE AFFIRMATION)

Live a life with less regret. That doesn't mean living a reckless life and doing what you want no matter how it affects others. It just means to enjoy the great moments in life and learn from the challenging moments. If we are being forced to grow, it's for a reason. Life won't always feel perfect but we can always look at life perfectly.

NeverStop.

I am grateful for these three things in my life

1. _____

2. _____

3. _____

I appreciate these two things about myself:

1. _____

2. _____

I am_____.
(POSITIVE AFFIRMATION)

We must be positive and optimistic. We need that from each other. If we are positive, we are able to look forward. If we are optimistic, we are able to believe that things can be better and improve. Without those two mindsets, it can be very difficult to make progress and accomplish our goals. Not impossible...but difficult. Be confident in the bigger plan more than your plan.

NeverStop.

I am grateful for these three things in my life

1. _____

2. _____

3. _____

I appreciate these two things about myself:

1. _____

2. _____

I am_____.
(POSITIVE AFFIRMATION)

Everybody needs somebody sometimes. Recognizing the value in others and asking for help is a strength, not a weakness. Giving to others is often easy to do but we aren't always good at receiving help. Work on becoming more grateful and humble while excepting help from others. Don't let it make you feel less or insecure. Always remember, some people show love by giving and acts of service. No one of us is better than all of us.

NeverStop.

I am grateful for these three things in my life

1. _____

2. _____

3. _____

I appreciate these two things about myself:

1. _____

2. _____

I am_____.
(POSITIVE AFFIRMATION)

We all need moments that make us slow down, and appreciate all of the great things we have in our lives. It's easy to get used to those things and ignore them but it's even easier to create a habit that makes you focus on how blessed you are. Want what you have, not what you think you need. Likely, you will realize you have always had all you need to be happy and grateful all along. Gain perspective, choose happiness, and be hopeful.

NeverStop.

I am grateful for these three things in my life

    1. _____

    2. _____

    3. _____

I appreciate these two things about myself:

    1. _____

    2. _____

I am_____.

                               (POSITIVE AFFIRMATION)

Cultivate serenity to accept the things we cannot change and the courage to change what we can. We can always control our thoughts, how we feel, how kind we are, how much we love, how much we give back and how we see the world. See the world as it could be and it will start to look like it should be. Be courageous and optimistic.

NeverStop.

I am grateful for these three things in my life

1. _____

2. _____

3. _____

I appreciate these two things about myself:

1. _____

2. _____

I am_____.
(POSITIVE AFFIRMATION)

We won't know our full potential until we push ourselves beyond our comfort zone. Put in the work, believe you can, and begin with the end in mind. When we set our minds to something, we can do some pretty great things. Our strength is greater than we know.

NeverStop.

I am grateful for these three things in my life

    1. _____

    2. _____

    3. _____

I appreciate these two things about myself:

    1. _____

    2. _____

I am_____.

                           (POSITIVE AFFIRMATION)

We should always remain curious, find happiness in the small things, and always work hard for what we want. Never get caught up in the day to day because time will fly by. Our minds goal is autopilot and survival but we can make it focus on improvement and thriving in life. Live a mindful life.

NeverStop.

I am grateful for these three things in my life

1. _____

2. _____

3. _____

I appreciate these two things about myself:

1. _____

2. _____

I am_____.
(POSITIVE AFFIRMATION)

Establish a healthy work life balance. Sometimes people work a lot because they feel good doing what they are good at while at work. It's essential to find things you love to do and make you feel fulfilled outside of work too. Our purpose goes well beyond our jobs. You are valuable, capable, and significant. Love to live life..

NeverStop.

I am grateful for these three things in my life

1. _____

2. _____

3. _____

I appreciate these two things about myself:

1. _____

2. _____

I am_____.

(POSITIVE AFFIRMATION)

Cultivate a deep sense of gratitude. Be grateful for things without needing the hardships or lack of things in our life. Don't only appreciate the sunshine on rainy days...take a moment to be thankful for the amazing things in our lives. The world is not against you, it is for you. Write down things you are grateful for every day. Choose your mindset. Be optimistic. Choose hope and faith.

NeverStop.

I am grateful for these three things in my life

1. _____

2. _____

3. _____

I appreciate these two things about myself:

1. _____

2. _____

I am_____.
(POSITIVE AFFIRMATION)

Never under estimate the power of a smile or a genuine thank you. Those two things instantly multiply when you send them out. Be a picture of happiness and gratitude and that will become the picture of how you see the world. It's always your choice. Choose love. Choose happiness.

NeverStop.

I am grateful for these three things in my life

    1. _____

    2. _____

    3. _____

I appreciate these two things about myself:

    1. _____

    2. _____

I am_____.

(POSITIVE AFFIRMATION)

Be more impressed by the way people treat other people and how they make the world a better place. Spend less time being impressed by looks, money, fame, cars, houses, etc. Show people who you are on the inside more often than what you are on the outside. Be good to others as often as you can.

NeverStop.

I am grateful for these three things in my life

1. _____

2. _____

3. _____

I appreciate these two things about myself:

1. _____

2. _____

I am_____.
(POSITIVE AFFIRMATION)

All that you can do or say is always enough. Develop the habit of giving and doing all that you can, not as little as you need to. The sweet spot is knowing that your best is enough and still wanting to do better. Be inspired by knowing that your effort always matters. Be patient. Be positive.

NeverStop.

I am grateful for these three things in my life

1. _____

2. _____

3. _____

I appreciate these two things about myself:

1. _____

2. _____

I am_____.
(POSITIVE AFFIRMATION)

The difference between stress and passion is how we think about our situation. Make sure your stress relievers don't cause stress an hour later. See stress as preparation for the great things coming your way. We stress because we care, not because we aren't capable to handle situations. Embrace stress and use it to sharpen your focus.

NeverStop.

I am grateful for these three things in my life

1. _____

2. _____

3. _____

I appreciate these two things about myself:

1. _____

2. _____

I am_____.
(POSITIVE AFFIRMATION)

Change and transformation take time and we must understand challenges are a part of the process. Our ability to rebound is our greatest attribute. We can get through time times and we can come out stronger than before. Persistence and optimism are key. Being transformed requires us to leave behind what we used to be and to be made new.

NeverStop.

I am grateful for these three things in my life

1. _____

2. _____

3. _____

I appreciate these two things about myself:

1. _____

2. _____

I am_____.

(POSITIVE AFFIRMATION)

Be in control of your emotions. Use your emotions to show how much you care, but don't let emotions use you. Don't feel like you have to have an emotional roller coaster on a daily basis. Understand your emotions and decide how they make you sound, look, and act. Attitude is more important than aptitude.

NeverStop.

I am grateful for these three things in my life

1. _____

2. _____

3. _____

I appreciate these two things about myself:

1. _____

2. _____

I am_____.

(POSITIVE AFFIRMATION)

Always keep your ego in your back pocket, not on your collar. Be confident in yourself because you have improved, not because you think you are better than others. We are all capable of making a difference. Lift up others while you are rising. Be humble. Be an example.

NeverStop.

I am grateful for these three things in my life

1. _____

2. _____

3. _____

I appreciate these two things about myself:

1. _____

2. _____

I am_____.
(POSITIVE AFFIRMATION)

Be careful that the desire to have something that someone else has doesn't take over the desire to have the actual thing. You will miss it when you get it if you are constantly looking to see what others have. Need what you have and want what you need. Be grateful for what we have.

NeverStop.

I am grateful for these three things in my life

1. _____

2. _____

3. _____

I appreciate these two things about myself:

1. _____

2. _____

I am_____.

(POSITIVE AFFIRMATION)

When your "why" is just something you want, "when", "what" and "where" will be barriers. When your "why" is a must, there are no barriers, only things you plan for. Wants show up in what we say but what we must have shows up in our actions. Develop self-awareness to fully understand your why. We are all inspired by something.

NeverStop.

I am grateful for these three things in my life

1. _____

2. _____

3. _____

I appreciate these two things about myself:

1. _____

2. _____

I am_____.

(POSITIVE AFFIRMATION)

It's never too late to pursue your goals, build that relationship, take that trip, or even just have a mindful conversation you have been needing to have. If your plan didn't work, change the plan, not the goal. Write down your goals and read them frequently. Set daily, weekly, monthly, yearly goals. Be grateful for the moments we have.

NeverStop.

I am grateful for these three things in my life

1. _____

2. _____

3. _____

I appreciate these two things about myself:

1. _____

2. _____

I am_____.
                                (POSITIVE AFFIRMATION)

Just when you think your happiness couldn't reach a new level, an amazing gift can come in to your life at any moment...if you let it. Don't let momentary challenges affect your lifelong happiness. Always be optimistic of what is to come. Look for things in your life that make you feel happy and grateful.

NeverStop.

I am grateful for these three things in my life

1. _____

2. _____

3. _____

I appreciate these two things about myself:

1. _____

2. _____

I am_____.
(POSITIVE AFFIRMATION)

Don't live in a life of fear and apprehension. Do not worry as much. Live a life of awareness and mindful decisions. Be excited about new opportunities we get every day. Make decisions based on what you want, not what you fear might happen. Most of the things we worry about don't happen. Be prepared for the worst, but always hope for the best.

NeverStop.

I am grateful for these three things in my life

1. _____

2. _____

3. _____

I appreciate these two things about myself:

1. _____

2. _____

I am_____.
(POSITIVE AFFIRMATION)

Be mindfully loyal. Being loyal isn't staying in a situation because you have to, it's about staying because you made a choice to. We all have the ability move on if something isn't good for our heart and soul. Make sure your habits of loyalty are good for you. Never settle for less than you deserve. Always know your value.

NeverStop.

I am grateful for these three things in my life

1. _____

2. _____

3. _____

I appreciate these two things about myself:

1. _____

2. _____

I am_____.
(POSITIVE AFFIRMATION)

If you feel like someone acts like they are better than you, understand that they may not feel like that at all. The real issue might be that you don't think you are as good as them. Evaluate yourself based on your progress and potential, not someone else's. Appreciate how far you have come and know that you are capable of amazing things. Be confident but never boast.

NeverStop.

I am grateful for these three things in my life

1. _____

2. _____

3. _____

I appreciate these two things about myself:

1. _____

2. _____

I am_____.
(POSITIVE AFFIRMATION)

Spend more time listening than you do talking. When we talk, we only say what we know. When we listen, we are able to learn new things. Listen to understand, not reply. Be excited about learning, it's a pretty great opportunity that we all have and shouldn't take for granted. See value in others and yourself. Be patient.

NeverStop.

I am grateful for these three things in my life

1. _____

2. _____

3. _____

I appreciate these two things about myself:

1. _____

2. _____

I am_____.

(POSITIVE AFFIRMATION)

Begin a pursuit of a goal with the end in mind. Visualize what accomplishing your goal looks like and believe in yourself that you can get there. We must first see the target before we can hit it. Believe in your abilities to overcome adversity while keeping that end goal in sight. Help others accomplish their goals along the way. Be patient. Be relentless.

NeverStop.

I am grateful for these three things in my life

1. _____

2. _____

3. _____

I appreciate these two things about myself:

1. _____

2. _____

I am_____.
(POSITIVE AFFIRMATION)

Spend more time studying yourself than you do others. No two hearts, minds, or bodies are the same. Observing others and then judging yourself will rarely lead to a sense of happiness. Feel great with where you are while pursuing where you want to go. You are always loved and are just the way you are meant to be in every moment.

NeverStop.

I am grateful for these three things in my life

1. _____

2. _____

3. _____

I appreciate these two things about myself:

1. _____

2. _____

I am_____.
(POSITIVE AFFIRMATION)

While our actions do matter, the spirit of that action is just as important. Having the spirit of generosity is more important than feeling obligated while being generous. The spirit of love while doing something for someone is more meaningful than loving because you feel like you have to. Be mindful of the spirit in which we do things. Be kind. Be humble.

NeverStop.

I am grateful for these three things in my life

1. _____

2. _____

3. _____

I appreciate these two things about myself:

1. _____

2. _____

I am_____.
(POSITIVE AFFIRMATION)

Being positive it a negative situation isn't being naive. It's a commitment to a positive mindset and can have an impact on those around us. It's easy to be positive when things are great but when they aren't and you can still be hopeful and optimistic, that is when others can see who you are. Always control your own thoughts. Under pressure, what is on the inside is what gets squeezed out of us. Be genuine. Be positive.

NeverStop.

I am grateful for these three things in my life

1. _____

2. _____

3. _____

I appreciate these two things about myself:

1. _____

2. _____

I am_____.

(POSITIVE AFFIRMATION)

Work on achieving a healthy balance of work and play. Do more per hour, not more hours. Working hours a day is good but working hours straight is not. We are the same person at home and work. We all need a balance in order to be great in both aspects of life. Do things that light the fire in your soul. Rejuvenate your body.

NeverStop.

I am grateful for these three things in my life

1. _____

2. _____

3. _____

I appreciate these two things about myself:

1. _____

2. _____

I am_____.

(POSITIVE AFFIRMATION)

Even when things get tough and they don't go as planned...It's the courage to keep going that counts. Tougher moments are character building moments that also provide an opportunity to gain a bigger perspective. When you are challenged, trust in yourself...You have gotten through every other challenge so far. Believe in your ability to endure. Be optimistic. Be disciplined.

NeverStop.

I am grateful for these three things in my life

1. _____

2. _____

3. _____

I appreciate these two things about myself:

1. _____

2. _____

I am_____.

(POSITIVE AFFIRMATION)

Don't get too caught up in counting the miles when you are trying to go the extra mile. The key is to just do all that you can and not see it as extra. Effort is everything. Don't count the cost along the way.

NeverStop.

I am grateful for these three things in my life

1. _____

2. _____

3. _____

I appreciate these two things about myself:

1. _____

2. _____

I am_____.
　　　　　　　　　(POSITIVE AFFIRMATION)

Always hope for the best for others. There is enough room, time, space, money, opportunity etc., for all of us to live a fulfilling life. Never try to benefit from someone else's misfortune. Lift people up and always reach out your hand with love. Life is precious.

NeverStop.

I am grateful for these three things in my life

1. _____

2. _____

3. _____

I appreciate these two things about myself:

1. _____

2. _____

I am_____.

(POSITIVE AFFIRMATION)

We control our own mindset. Learn to see obstacles, failures, and challenges as motivation. Our mindset dictates how we see the world. Other people will have different perspectives but you can always have your own. We all control how we respond so don't give that control to others. Be hopeful and optimistic. Be strong in Faith. . Never stop.

NeverStop.

I am grateful for these three things in my life

    1. _____

    2. _____

    3. _____

I appreciate these two things about myself:

    1. _____

    2. _____

I am_____.
                      (POSITIVE AFFIRMATION)

It is important to realize when we are over complicating things in life. Always remember that the things that are easy to do are also the things easy not to do. Be disciplined and focused enough to do the easy things that prepare you for the difficult things. Do the things today that you'll be glad you did tomorrow. Be sober minded and open hearted. . Never stop.

NeverStop.

I am grateful for these three things in my life

1. _____

2. _____

3. _____

I appreciate these two things about myself:

1. _____

2. _____

I am_____.
(POSITIVE AFFIRMATION)

Take complete ownership for your mistakes. Think to give everyone credit when you succeed. Don't point fingers or find excuses if you make a mistake... Just own it and learn from it. People will trust you more when you take accountability and don't make excuses. No one is perfect so don't feel like you have to be. Be humble.

NeverStop.

I am grateful for these three things in my life

1. _____

2. _____

3. _____

I appreciate these two things about myself:

1. _____

2. _____

I am_____.
(POSITIVE AFFIRMATION)

We will find the things in the direction that we are looking. If you spend too much time looking backwards, you may miss the great things that are right in front of you. Spend more time looking at your goals and less time looking at the past and the lessons learned. If we looks for things to be grateful for, we will always find them.

NeverStop.

I am grateful for these three things in my life

1. _____

2. _____

3. _____

I appreciate these two things about myself:

1. _____

2. _____

I am_____.

(POSITIVE AFFIRMATION)

We don't need much to live a happy and fulfilling life. In fact, it's not found in getting more things or accomplishing more...It is simply found in the way we think about the things we already have and the life we get to live. The decision to live a happy life is yours to make. Intrinsic happiness cannot be taken from us.

NeverStop.

I am grateful for these three things in my life

1. _____

2. _____

3. _____

I appreciate these two things about myself:

1. _____

2. _____

I am_____.
(POSITIVE AFFIRMATION)

The truth is elegantly simple. Be honest with yourself and with others. Take responsibility for your actions when you do them, not just if you get caught. Say thank you to those that offer moments of grace instead of feeling like you always have to say sorry. Honesty builds trust and is an act of love. Be patient.

NeverStop.

I am grateful for these three things in my life

1. _____

2. _____

3. _____

I appreciate these two things about myself:

1. _____

2. _____

I am_____.

(POSITIVE AFFIRMATION)

Find a balance between humility and self-esteem. Be confident in yourself but never boast. The goal is to be the best version of yourself not better than anyone else. Be confident in your ability to help others and your ability to be good to others.

NeverStop.

I am grateful for these three things in my life

1. _____

2. _____

3. _____

I appreciate these two things about myself:

1. _____

2. _____

I am_____.
(POSITIVE AFFIRMATION)

Kind words or actions go a long way. You never know what kind of day someone is having and you never know what kind of impact you can have. Be good to others without the expectation of getting anything in return. Focus on being good more than being right. Give more than you receive.

NeverStop.

I am grateful for these three things in my life

1. _____

2. _____

3. _____

I appreciate these two things about myself:

1. _____

2. _____

I am_____.
(POSITIVE AFFIRMATION)

Have higher expectations for yourself than others have for you. Hold yourself accountable. Only you know your true potential. Hold yourself to a higher standard because it is who you are.

Recognize opportunities to use your gifts.

NeverStop.

I am grateful for these three things in my life

1. _____

2. _____

3. _____

I appreciate these two things about myself:

1. _____

2. _____

I am_____.

(POSITIVE AFFIRMATION)

When we are trying to pursue something more or make a change in our lives, moving forward typically isn't the hardest part. The first step to moving forward is letting go of what is holding us back. That is usually the hardest part but it's the most important. We all have the ability to change and control our thoughts and behaviors.

NeverStop.

I am grateful for these three things in my life

1. _____

2. _____

3. _____

I appreciate these two things about myself:

1. _____

2. _____

I am_____.
(POSITIVE AFFIRMATION)

Cultivate a belief that the future is going to be even better than the present. Have high expectations for yourself and for each day. Practice optimism by developing an unwavering belief in your future. Never lower your expectations. If you want an area of life to improve, it will never come from lowering expectations.

NeverStop.

I am grateful for these three things in my life

1. _____

2. _____

3. _____

I appreciate these two things about myself:

1. _____

2. _____

I am_____.
(POSITIVE AFFIRMATION)

A negative mind will never lead to a positive life. If you find yourself surrounded by negativity, it can feel heavy and restraining. If you find yourself around positivity it is inspiring, freeing and uplifting. Either we are a product of our environment or our environment is a product of us.
Make a decision to be positive, optimistic, and grateful.

NeverStop.

I am grateful for these three things in my life

1. _____

2. _____

3. _____

I appreciate these two things about myself:

1. _____

2. _____

I am_____.

(POSITIVE AFFIRMATION)

Fact of life...things won't always go the way we planned but they will always turn out how it is meant to be. When we are humbled, it is a test of what is in our hearts. Typically, those moments are also a turning point in our lives. Embrace the challenges in life and know it is out of love to prepare us for the great things to come. Learn and grow.

NeverStop.

I am grateful for these three things in my life

1. _____

2. _____

3. _____

I appreciate these two things about myself:

1. _____

2. _____

I am_____.
(POSITIVE AFFIRMATION)

The best way to say what we want to say is to act in a mindful way. Actions show how we really feel while words can sometimes reflect how we wished we felt. Back up your words with your actions. Find ways, on a daily basis, to show someone how you feel. Our words sometimes just go through the mind while our actions go straight to the heart. Reflect what you want to receive.

NeverStop.

I am grateful for these three things in my life

1. _____
2. _____
3. _____

I appreciate these two things about myself:

1. _____
2. _____

I am_____.
                    (POSITIVE AFFIRMATION)

Sometimes we need to slow down take a deep breath. Today, take a moment to say thank you to someone that you are grateful for. Also, take a moment to tell someone that you love them and appreciate them. Not just thinking about the words, but thinking about how those people make you feel in your heart and soul. Love because we are loved.

NeverStop.

I am grateful for these three things in my life

1. _____

2. _____

3. _____

I appreciate these two things about myself:

1. _____

2. _____

I am_____.
(POSITIVE AFFIRMATION)

Resting to prepare for something is different than resting to avoid something. Rest and sleep is critical to good health but make sure it doesn't take over the time you need to be working hard. It's the moments when you don't feel like doing something is when it is most beneficial to do it. Be excited about life. Focus on your why. Live a mindful life.

NeverStop.

I am grateful for these three things in my life

1. _____

2. _____

3. _____

I appreciate these two things about myself:

1. _____

2. _____

I am_____.

(POSITIVE AFFIRMATION)

Never be too proud to ask for help. It is better to show humility, admit you don't know the answers, and ask questions. It is better to look like a fool for a moment instead never asking the question and look like a fool for lifetime. Asking for help is a sign of strength, not weakness. Be humble. Be positive.

NeverStop.

I am grateful for these three things in my life

1. _____

2. _____

3. _____

I appreciate these two things about myself:

1. _____

2. _____

I am_____.

(POSITIVE AFFIRMATION)

Don't be so busy being busy that you miss the fulfilling joys of life. Focus more on the great things in our lives, not our problems. Do what you love. Do what you have always wanted to do and be the person you have always wanted to be. Think differently and create new mindful daily routines.

NeverStop.

I am grateful for these three things in my life

1. _____

2. _____

3. _____

I appreciate these two things about myself:

1. _____

2. _____

I am_____.

(POSITIVE AFFIRMATION)

The first step of changing our lives is the self-awareness of the limiting belief that we have about ourselves or our situation. Think about when that limiting belief was developed and realize that it was based on who you used to be. Expand and grow your hearts and minds, take chances and find out your full potential. Be courageous.

NeverStop.

I am grateful for these three things in my life

1. _____

2. _____

3. _____

I appreciate these two things about myself:

1. _____

2. _____

I am_____.
(POSITIVE AFFIRMATION)

The difference between being committed to a goal versus just wanting a goal is that when you are completely committed, you are not willing to tolerate excuses. Don't look for reasons why you can't accomplish something...That is based on the past, not the future. Instead, focus on the reason why you started in the first place..

NeverStop.

I am grateful for these three things in my life

1. _____

2. _____

3. _____

I appreciate these two things about myself:

1. _____

2. _____

I am_____.

(POSITIVE AFFIRMATION)

Make the choice of discipline over procrastination. The opportunities we have in front of us now may not be there later. Never underestimate the power of consistent discipline. The reward for a lack of discipline is immediate. The reward for consistent steadfast discipline lasts a lifetime. You are strong and able.

NeverStop.

I am grateful for these three things in my life

1. _____

2. _____

3. _____

I appreciate these two things about myself:

1. _____

2. _____

I am_____.
(POSITIVE AFFIRMATION)

Invest in yourself. Like most investments, daily commitments and patience pays off in the long run. You are worth the investment. Eat healthy, expand your mind by reading, exercise to strengthen your body and meditate to calm your mind. We all have habits...Make sure yours are aligned with loving yourself and knowing your worth.

NeverStop.

I am grateful for these three things in my life

1. _____

2. _____

3. _____

I appreciate these two things about myself:

1. _____

2. _____

I am_____.

(POSITIVE AFFIRMATION)

Love people for who they are. Not just for who they used to be, who you think they should be, or who they are going to be. Love in the moment and be grateful for each other in all moments. Love others how you would want to be loved. Never judge anyone. Soften your heart. Cultivate mindful relationships.

NeverStop.

I am grateful for these three things in my life

1. _____

2. _____

3. _____

I appreciate these two things about myself:

1. _____

2. _____

I am_____.
(POSITIVE AFFIRMATION)

Expand your mind to seek more than instant gratification. Easy come, easy go. Don't always look for shortcuts or the path of least resistance. The resistance is what makes us stronger and prepared for the amazing things to come. Love the process of earning the things you want...Not just getting it. Be patient with yourself and your journey.

NeverStop.

I am grateful for these three things in my life

1. _____

2. _____

3. _____

I appreciate these two things about myself:

1. _____

2. _____

I am_____.
(POSITIVE AFFIRMATION)

Don't be anxious about how long things take in life. Don't count the minutes because you could miss the moments. If you get anxious with how long it will take, always know it will take as long as it needs to. Use the time being demanded of you to learn and appreciate your journey. Great things take time.

NeverStop.

I am grateful for these three things in my life

1. _____

2. _____

3. _____

I appreciate these two things about myself:

1. _____

2. _____

I am_____.

(POSITIVE AFFIRMATION)

Spend some time differentiating between your goals and strategies. If you don't meet your goals, don't lower them... Instead, improve your strategy. When we find the right strategy, the goals will seem easier to accomplish. You are able to accomplish whatever you want with the right strategy. Be patient. Believe in yourself. Learn from failures and success..

NeverStop.

I am grateful for these three things in my life

1. _____

2. _____

3. _____

I appreciate these two things about myself:

1. _____

2. _____

I am_____.

(POSITIVE AFFIRMATION)

Choose your mindset. Don't allow others to decide that for you. Make up your mind with how you are going to think about life. Learn from the past, be tremendously grateful for where you are today, and optimistically look forward to where you are going. Don't be anxious about the future, be excited about it. Know that you were made to be of power, love, and self-discipline.

NeverStop.

I am grateful for these three things in my life

1. _____

2. _____

3. _____

I appreciate these two things about myself:

1. _____

2. _____

I am_____.

(POSITIVE AFFIRMATION)

Don't get too caught up in over thinking. If we wait until we know everything before we do something, we may never do anything. If an opportunity comes your way, and it excites you, take a risk and trust that you can learn and can be good at whatever you want to. You may be surprised with how much you are capable of. Put in the work and trust yourself.

NeverStop.

I am grateful for these three things in my life

1. _____

2. _____

3. _____

I appreciate these two things about myself:

1. _____

2. _____

I am_____.
(POSITIVE AFFIRMATION)

See the best in people because most people don't see the best in themselves. A few kind words can change the hearts of those around us. Be a reflection of love and appreciation. Be one of the reasons why someone smiles today. Be the first one to smile...It's contagious.

NeverStop.

I am grateful for these three things in my life

1. _____

2. _____

3. _____

I appreciate these two things about myself:

1. _____

2. _____

I am_____.
(POSITIVE AFFIRMATION)

People may let you down and you may let yourself down. In those moments of disappointment, cultivate a sense of hope. Hope beyond wishful thinking but for a desire for something better. Offer each other, and yourself, moments of grace. Forgive and grow.

NeverStop.

I am grateful for these three things in my life

1. _____

2. _____

3. _____

I appreciate these two things about myself:

1. _____

2. _____

I am_____.
(POSITIVE AFFIRMATION)

When we run out of energy or motivation, we are probably focusing on how much effort it is going to take or what we will have to sacrifice to accomplish our goal. In those moments, refocus on your "why" and be inspired by why you started in the first place. Be hopeful and focus on your why, you will always find enough energy and motivation. Great things take time.

NeverStop.

I am grateful for these three things in my life

1. _____

2. _____

3. _____

I appreciate these two things about myself:

1. _____

2. _____

I am_____.

(POSITIVE AFFIRMATION)

Don't spend your life trying to make everyone else happy. We can provide each other with moments of joy but authentic, steadfast happiness has to come from within each one of us. Happiness is a choice and a daily decision.

NeverStop.

I am grateful for these three things in my life

1. _____

2. _____

3. _____

I appreciate these two things about myself:

1. _____

2. _____

I am_____.
(POSITIVE AFFIRMATION)

Some of the most surprising, unexpected, challenging things that happen in life redirect us to the best thing in our lives. If you are going through a challenging time, trust the divine nature of all things and know that He is already on the other side of that challenge. Believe it before you see it.

NeverStop.

I am grateful for these three things in my life

1. _____

2. _____

3. _____

I appreciate these two things about myself:

1. _____

2. _____

I am_____.

(POSITIVE AFFIRMATION)

Sometimes things take a while to happen in our lives. However, when it does happen, we will be thankful that we were patient while waiting. Sometimes we have develop ourselves before we get what we desire. Who we become along the way is more fulfilling than the desire itself. His timing is always perfect. Everything will happen exactly when it is meant to.

NeverStop.

I am grateful for these three things in my life

1. _____

2. _____

3. _____

I appreciate these two things about myself:

1. _____

2. _____

I am_____.

(POSITIVE AFFIRMATION)

Sometimes it seems like people come in to our life by accident but we must put the effort in to have them stay in our life on purpose. Cultivate meaningful relationships and be grateful for the hearts of those around us. Expand your heart and mind.

NeverStop.

I am grateful for these three things in my life

1. _____

2. _____

3. _____

I appreciate these two things about myself:

1. _____

2. _____

I am_____.
(POSITIVE AFFIRMATION)

Our value has nothing to do with the house we live in, car we drive, or job we have. Measure our value by what's on the inside, not what material things other can see. We have all been made for a unique purpose and that makes us valuable beyond measure. See your value and the value of those around us. Love yourself, love your neighbor.

NeverStop.

I am grateful for these three things in my life

1. _____

2. _____

3. _____

I appreciate these two things about myself:

1. _____

2. _____

I am_____.
                      (POSITIVE AFFIRMATION)

We must understand that we can always learn more. We are changing each day and the world is always changing. Never lose that hunger to want to ask more questions than you can answer. No one knows it all. The more we see in life, we will realize the less we know. Be humble. Be patient. Be open minded. Seek wisdom.

NeverStop.

I am grateful for these three things in my life

1. _____

2. _____

3. _____

I appreciate these two things about myself:

1. _____

2. _____

I am_____.

(POSITIVE AFFIRMATION)

Sometimes we have to take a risk in life. Understand the risks and develop a strategy. Don't always play it safe. Change the strategy but never the goal you have been wanting to accomplish. This blessing of a life is short and goes by fast. Learn from mistakes. Challenge yourself. Push your limits.

NeverStop.

I am grateful for these three things in my life

1. _____

2. _____

3. _____

I appreciate these two things about myself:

1. _____

2. _____

I am_____.
(POSITIVE AFFIRMATION)

Allow the mystery of life to inspire and encourage you every day. Don't let uncertainty cause you to worry. Worrying doesn't do much good most of the time anyway. Focus more on what could go right instead of worrying about what could go wrong. See each day as another opportunity to fulfill your potential and pursue your purpose.

NeverStop.

I am grateful for these three things in my life

1. _____

2. _____

3. _____

I appreciate these two things about myself:

1. _____

2. _____

I am_____.

(POSITIVE AFFIRMATION)

Control your emotions. Don't allow others to control them for you. You are in charge of your thoughts, beliefs, actions, and your perspective. Never choose anger or revenge. Choose love and forgiveness. Decide who you want to be in your life and always know you are able to let go and grow.

NeverStop.

I am grateful for these three things in my life

1. _____

2. _____

3. _____

I appreciate these two things about myself:

1. _____

2. _____

I am_____.

(POSITIVE AFFIRMATION)

Never be too proud to ask for help. No one does everything on their own. We all need help or guidance along the way. Asking for help shows that you value others, not that you aren't capable. Sometimes people show love by offering help so don't be threatened, see it as a display of love.

NeverStop.

I am grateful for these three things in my life

1. _____

2. _____

3. _____

I appreciate these two things about myself:

1. _____

2. _____

I am_____.
(POSITIVE AFFIRMATION)

True happiness is to enjoy the present moment without being anxious and dependent upon the future. Don't be distracted with hopes or fears, be satisfied with what we have and realize it is sufficient. Find harmony in knowing that all of us are right where we are meant to be. Things will happen when we are ready for them to happen. Cherish every moment.

NeverStop.

I am grateful for these three things in my life

1. _____
2. _____
3. _____

I appreciate these two things about myself:

1. _____
2. _____

I am_____.
(POSITIVE AFFIRMATION)

Learn to be happy with the simple things and it will be simple to be happy. Being happy is a choice and a mindset. Happiness begins with gratitude. Gratitude begins with awareness. Focus more on what we have, not what we wish we had. Raise your standards and develop daily habits to cultivate gratefulness. Be inspired by our blessings.

NeverStop.

I am grateful for these three things in my life

1. _____

2. _____

3. _____

I appreciate these two things about myself:

1. _____

2. _____

I am_____.
(POSITIVE AFFIRMATION)

Speak with a positive mindset to yourself and to others. Instead of thinking what we shouldn't do, think more about what we should be doing. Focus more on what you want, not what you don't want. Live in a state of fullness, not lack. Look for the positive aspects of life. When you get the opportunity to change, think of what you gain, not what you could lose..

NeverStop.

I am grateful for these three things in my life

1. _____

2. _____

3. _____

I appreciate these two things about myself:

1. _____

2. _____

I am_____.

(POSITIVE AFFIRMATION)

In order to let go of what was, we need to gain perspective of what is and what can be. Sometimes the answer is just move on but there is also a time to persevere. Let go of the things weighing you down so that you can run this race of life given to us. Be grateful for the lessons learned that inspire us and helped us grow. The goal is progress so love yourself along the way.

NeverStop.

I am grateful for these three things in my life

1. _____

2. _____

3. _____

I appreciate these two things about myself:

1. _____

2. _____

I am_____.
(POSITIVE AFFIRMATION)

We must understand that changing something in our life doesn't always take a long time. Sometimes it just starts with one decision. Allow your heart and mind to expand and be transformed. Be the owner of your life and pursue your purpose. Change the way you think about things and those things in life will change.

NeverStop.

I am grateful for these three things in my life

1. _____

2. _____

3. _____

I appreciate these two things about myself:

1. _____

2. _____

I am_____.

(POSITIVE AFFIRMATION)

Live by choice, not by chance. Listen to your own inner voice more than you listen to the voice of others. Only you know what you have been through and where you want to go. Be motivated, not manipulated. Trust in yourself.

NeverStop.

I am grateful for these three things in my life

1. _____

2. _____

3. _____

I appreciate these two things about myself:

1. _____

2. _____

I am_____.

(POSITIVE AFFIRMATION)

Everyone we meet and interact with is somebody's somebody. We are all somebody's person. Be kind. Be considerate. Lift up others by giving and shining your light. Don't put other people's light out so that your light is brighter...there is plenty of room in this world for more light to shine. Do what lights that fire in your soul, soften your heart, smile more often.

NeverStop.

I am grateful for these three things in my life

1. _____

2. _____

3. _____

I appreciate these two things about myself:

1. _____

2. _____

I am_____.
(POSITIVE AFFIRMATION)

Don't be so busy trying to prove your point that you actually miss the point. It's better to be kind than to always feel like you have to be right. Being right is perception, but being kind is a fact. No one knows everything about everything. Talk TO people, not AT people. Offer moments of grace, admit mistakes we make, and cultivate mindful relationships that lift up our hearts.

NeverStop.

I am grateful for these three things in my life

1. _____

2. _____

3. _____

I appreciate these two things about myself:

1. _____

2. _____

I am_____.
(POSITIVE AFFIRMATION)

Become comfortable being uncomfortable. Push beyond your limits. We will never procrastinate our way to success. Life awards us with experiences after we have put in the work. Discomfort causes growth and forces us to be mindful to find a way to improve. Embrace the challenges that come in life because they are meant for us in a divine way.

NeverStop.

I am grateful for these three things in my life

1. _____

2. _____

3. _____

I appreciate these two things about myself:

1. _____

2. _____

I am_____.
(POSITIVE AFFIRMATION)

A day unused is lost...a word unsaid is lost...talent unused is lost...abilities unused are lost...ideas not shared are lost. Every day matters, your words and ideas matter, your talents and abilities matter. Be around people that make your life better and find ways to make a difference to those around us. Take advantage of the day. Carpe diem.

NeverStop.

I am grateful for these three things in my life

1. _____

2. _____

3. _____

I appreciate these two things about myself:

1. _____

2. _____

I am_____.

(POSITIVE AFFIRMATION)

Sometimes, in order to grow, we have to just let some things go. Accept the things we can't change as those things can often change us. Be flexible with thoughts and actions but rigid in values. Never judge those around us or keep a count of wrong doings. Cultivate a progressive mindset.

NeverStop.

I am grateful for these three things in my life

1. _____
2. _____
3. _____

I appreciate these two things about myself:

1. _____
2. _____

I am_____.
(POSITIVE AFFIRMATION)

Take advantage of the opportunities we are blessed with in life. Sometimes those opportunities will look like work but we must see the result we will get after we put the work in. If it scares you, it is probably worth giving it your best. Move beyond your comfort zone. Embracing one opportunity often leads to more opportunities.

NeverStop.

I am grateful for these three things in my life

1. _____

2. _____

3. _____

I appreciate these two things about myself:

1. _____

2. _____

I am_____.
(POSITIVE AFFIRMATION)

We all have the ability to create something magnificent in this world without having to ask permission or get approval from those around us. Do things that spark the fire inside you more than the fire around you. Use your divine gifts and make a difference in the world by just being you. Be courageous. We are able to do great things.

NeverStop.

I am grateful for these three things in my life

1. _____

2. _____

3. _____

I appreciate these two things about myself:

1. _____

2. _____

I am_____.

(POSITIVE AFFIRMATION)

Take action in your life. Don't just worry about things in your life, do something about them. Write down the things you worry about and figure out a plan to do something about it. Most of the things we worry about don't even end up happening. Believe in yourself and know that you are strong, capable, and significant.

NeverStop.

I am grateful for these three things in my life

1. _____

2. _____

3. _____

I appreciate these two things about myself:

1. _____

2. _____

I am_____.
(POSITIVE AFFIRMATION)

Don't always focusing on being a go getter...we must also be a go giver. We become more inspired when we give than when we get. What we give out to the world will come back to us even more. Doing good things for others encourages others to do good for others. Give without expectations of getting. Give patience, give optimism, give effort, give hope, give faith, and give love.

NeverStop.

I am grateful for these three things in my life

1. _____

2. _____

3. _____

I appreciate these two things about myself:

1. _____

2. _____

I am_____.
                              (POSITIVE AFFIRMATION)

One way to learn how to do things right is to do things wrong. Keep your head up and take pride in effort, not just always succeeding. Adversity teaches us much more than success. Keep in that mind while cultivating relationships with those around us. Offer each other moments of Grace and make it ok to make mistakes. Be humble. Be persistent.

NeverStop.

I am grateful for these three things in my life

    1. _____

    2. _____

    3. _____

I appreciate these two things about myself:

    1. _____

    2. _____

I am_____.
                        (POSITIVE AFFIRMATION)

Truth is, we cannot avoid the future. However, we can move away from our past. Don't spend too much time looking in the rear view mirror, we aren't going that way. Be inspired by fulfilling your potential. Be transformed in heart, mind, and soul. What has happened in life has prepared us for the amazing things are to come. Love to live life.

NeverStop.

I am grateful for these three things in my life

1. _____

2. _____

3. _____

I appreciate these two things about myself:

1. _____

2. _____

I am_____.

(POSITIVE AFFIRMATION)

Be accountable for the energy of your life. For the way you think about life determines how you treat yourself and those around you. Don't blame others or circumstances. Find peace in knowing that things happen in life but they aren't just happening to you. The way we respond will determine the outcome.

NeverStop.

I am grateful for these three things in my life

1. _____

2. _____

3. _____

I appreciate these two things about myself:

1. _____

2. _____

I am_____.
(POSITIVE AFFIRMATION)

Knowing that we all have possibilities and opportunities should always be seen as a luxury to us. Love to live life. Believe in yourself and share your divine gifts. We are all able to learn and grow. Be patient. Be grateful.

NeverStop.

I am grateful for these three things in my life

1. _____

2. _____

3. _____

I appreciate these two things about myself:

1. _____

2. _____

I am_____.

(POSITIVE AFFIRMATION)

Never have too much pride to not be able to admit when you are wrong. While we are doing our best, we will not always be right...and that's ok. No one is always right so don't stress when you aren't. That's just an opportunity to learn and grow. We all need help and structure. No one of us is better than all of us. Be humble. Forgive because we have been forgiven.

NeverStop.

I am grateful for these three things in my life

1. _____

2. _____

3. _____

I appreciate these two things about myself:

1. _____

2. _____

I am_____.
(POSITIVE AFFIRMATION)

No matter what we may go through, never give up. Be optimistic and trust that great things are coming our way. Adversity provides unique perspective for when we overcome the challenge, we are able to see how much we have grown. Your effort always matters. Don't compare yourself to others, we are all on our own journey. Always know your value.

NeverStop.

I am grateful for these three things in my life

1. _____

2. _____

3. _____

I appreciate these two things about myself:

1. _____

2. _____

I am_____.
(POSITIVE AFFIRMATION)

No one can do everything but everyone can do something. Always remember your something is always enough and is valued by more people than you know. Keep doing your something with everything you have. In the end, we will never wish we gave less effort. Little things add up to be the big things.

NeverStop.

I am grateful for these three things in my life

1. _____

2. _____

3. _____

I appreciate these two things about myself:

1. _____

2. _____

I am_____.
(POSITIVE AFFIRMATION)

The old saying goes monkey see, monkey do... Notice, it isn't monkey hear, monkey do. The people we have been blessed with in our lives, often mimic our behaviors. Inspire others with our actions not just our words. See this as an opportunity to be a positive influence. No one is perfect, so don't feel like you have to be. Look like kindness, humility, and patience.

NeverStop.

I am grateful for these three things in my life

1. _____

2. _____

3. _____

I appreciate these two things about myself:

1. _____

2. _____

I am_____.

(POSITIVE AFFIRMATION)

Never burn any bridges in life. We never know where our journey will lead us. Cultivate meaningful relationships along the way, forgive and never hold grudges, always remember everyone is on a journey designed just for them. We have all been made in His image.

NeverStop.

I am grateful for these three things in my life

1. _____

2. _____

3. _____

I appreciate these two things about myself:

1. _____

2. _____

I am_____.
(POSITIVE AFFIRMATION)

Sometimes we need to let go of the things we are most afraid to lose. Learn to trust and not feel like we have to hold everything up. The first step to moving forward is a decision that you want to be somewhere else. Our minds control our actions. Be patient with yourself and pursue your purpose.

NeverStop.

I am grateful for these three things in my life

1. _____

2. _____

3. _____

I appreciate these two things about myself:

1. _____

2. _____

I am_____.
(POSITIVE AFFIRMATION)

Our hearts will be searched and our minds will be tested. This happens to make us see the direction of our life. We are tested and searched because we are loved. The direction of our life determines our destination. See the opportunity and His presence in all things.

NeverStop.

I am grateful for these three things in my life

1. _____

2. _____

3. _____

I appreciate these two things about myself:

1. _____

2. _____

I am_____.
(POSITIVE AFFIRMATION)

People should be seen as opportunities to improve...never obligations or burdens. The people in our lives are meant to be there. All of those around us give us opportunities to be more nice, to be more patient, to be more thoughtful, to be more loving, and to be more forgiving. Be more of all of the beautiful things you already are. Love the divine opportunities we have been blessed with.

NeverStop.

I am grateful for these three things in my life

1. _____

2. _____

3. _____

I appreciate these two things about myself:

1. _____

2. _____

I am_____.
(POSITIVE AFFIRMATION)

Don't get too caught up in thinking a fulfilling life has a look...not a car, not a house, not an income. Don't desire those things so much that you lose your value. People will always remember how we made them feel, not what car we drove or name brand of clothes we wore. You are what is valuable to people, not the items.

NeverStop.

I am grateful for these three things in my life

1. _____

2. _____

3. _____

I appreciate these two things about myself:

1. _____

2. _____

I am_____.
(POSITIVE AFFIRMATION)

Be the change you want to see in the world. Before we can be an influence on others, we must start doing the right thing ourselves. Be accountable for you thoughts, actions, words. If you want to see more love in the world, be more loving. The Spirit within us will inspire those around us.

NeverStop.

I am grateful for these three things in my life

1. _____

2. _____

3. _____

I appreciate these two things about myself:

1. _____

2. _____

I am_____.

(POSITIVE AFFIRMATION)

We must work on developing patience. When we are forced to wait for something, that time is used to strengthen our heart and mind. Sometimes certain opportunities will take a long time to develop but they will take as long as they need to. Opportunities that come too soon can cause difficulties. Be in a hurry to become more patient.

NeverStop.

I am grateful for these three things in my life

1. _____

2. _____

3. _____

I appreciate these two things about myself:

1. _____

2. _____

I am_____.

(POSITIVE AFFIRMATION)

Be steadfast with faith in fate. What is meant for us, will be true. No decision we make or change in circumstance will ever change that. Nothing will get in the way of our destined, divine purpose. Each moment is meant specifically for us to prepare us for the next. Cherish each moment of the process of life.

NeverStop.

I am grateful for these three things in my life

1. _____

2. _____

3. _____

I appreciate these two things about myself:

1. _____

2. _____

I am_____.

(POSITIVE AFFIRMATION)

Take time to be thankful for all that you have. We could have more but we could also have less. Train your mind to look for things you are grateful for and you will begin to see more of those things. Never want something more than you need it. Find heart happiness in things that cannot be taken from you. Fill your life with moments, not things. See the beauty of this world and the blessings all around us.

NeverStop.

I am grateful for these three things in my life

1. _____

2. _____

3. _____

I appreciate these two things about myself:

1. _____

2. _____

I am_____.
(POSITIVE AFFIRMATION)

The things we struggle with the most prepare us and lead us to the most fulfilling life. When we struggle, we are forced to look inside ourselves and find new strength. Struggle also makes us look for more meaning in life. Be steadfast and strong. Develop the endurance to run the race of life. Believe that you can make it through anything.

NeverStop.

I am grateful for these three things in my life

1. _____

2. _____

3. _____

I appreciate these two things about myself:

1. _____

2. _____

I am_____.
  (POSITIVE AFFIRMATION)

Love unconditionally. To love is a choice not a chore. Learn to love because that is who you are, not something that someone has earned from you. Don't keep tabs of wrong doings or mistakes, we all make them. Soften your heart and open your mind. Be love. Show love. Look like love. We love because he first loved us.

NeverStop.

I am grateful for these three things in my life

1. _____

2. _____

3. _____

I appreciate these two things about myself:

1. _____

2. _____

I am_____.
(POSITIVE AFFIRMATION)

Learn to not take things so personally. Other people's actions and thoughts are not because of you...it's their choice. Ignore the opinion of others since that is just a projection of their limitations or view of reality. It's isn't fact. Love yourself. Know your worth. Trust that you are significant and deeply loved.

NeverStop.

I am grateful for these three things in my life

1. _____
2. _____
3. _____

I appreciate these two things about myself:

1. _____
2. _____

I am_____.
(POSITIVE AFFIRMATION)

Our words and thoughts matter to those around us. Before you say what is on your mind...ask yourself three questions...is it kind? Is it true? Is it necessary? Always remember to slow down enough to speak with intent not just out of habit. Be comfortable with moments of silence and allow time for thought. Listen to understand, not reply. Show value to those around you.
Choose patience.

NeverStop.

I am grateful for these three things in my life

1. _____

2. _____

3. _____

I appreciate these two things about myself:

1. _____

2. _____

I am_____.
(POSITIVE AFFIRMATION)

Instead of thinking of a reason why you cannot accomplish your goal, think of one reason why you can... think of one reason why you should...and think of one reason why you must.

Consistently work on developing belief and confidence in yourself. Work hard, be optimistic, and focus on your why.

NeverStop.

I am grateful for these three things in my life

1. _____

2. _____

3. _____

I appreciate these two things about myself:

1. _____

2. _____

I am_____.

(POSITIVE AFFIRMATION)

Get up early. Invest in your health, mind, and soul. Do something you believe in. Do work that you love to do. Cultivate meaningful relationships that inspire you and improve your life. Try not to get too distracted looking forward to the next thing that you miss how much of a blessing your life already is.

NeverStop.

I am grateful for these three things in my life

1. _____

2. _____

3. _____

I appreciate these two things about myself:

1. _____

2. _____

I am_____.

(POSITIVE AFFIRMATION)

Feeling "stuck" is a decision. Don't be bound to the past. We all have the ability to move and grow. We are never stuck. Know that you have the right to your future. Never settle or feel like you don't deserve to be happy or fulfilled. He is the strength within us. Be brave. Have courage. Be respectful of yourself.

NeverStop.

I am grateful for these three things in my life

1. _____

2. _____

3. _____

I appreciate these two things about myself:

1. _____

2. _____

I am_____.

(POSITIVE AFFIRMATION)

Get in the habit of doing more than what is expected. Give life all you have. Don't settle for doing "just enough". Get in the habit of raising and maintaining your standards. Look at life differently and it will begin to look different. We cheat ourselves when we give less than we can.

NeverStop.

I am grateful for these three things in my life

1. _____

2. _____

3. _____

I appreciate these two things about myself:

1. _____

2. _____

I am_____.
(POSITIVE AFFIRMATION)

Walk in a manner with all humility and gentleness, with patience, with love for one another, and eagerness to maintain the Spirit in the sense of peace. Be so full of these things on the inside that people see it on the outside. You never know when a smile or a kind word could change someone's day. Make a difference today.

NeverStop.

I am grateful for these three things in my life

1. _____

2. _____

3. _____

I appreciate these two things about myself:

1. _____

2. _____

I am_____.
(POSITIVE AFFIRMATION)

Our energy is infectious. See that as an opportunity, not a burden. Those around us will give us the energy we give them. Improve your mind and choose your own thoughts. Growing and giving will inspire us and those around us. Choose your own thoughts that will turn into your actions. Smile often. Choose love. Choose optimism. Choose gratitude.

NeverStop.

I am grateful for these three things in my life

1. _____

2. _____

3. _____

I appreciate these two things about myself:

1. _____

2. _____

I am_____.
(POSITIVE AFFIRMATION)

Learn to trust and believe that you already have everything you need inside of you to live a fulfilling life. We just need to learn to peel back the layers and uncover what is covering our true potential. It is the uncovering process that allows us to recognize that we have the capacity to be transformed and ability to improve. Each moment is designed for us to prepare us for the next.

NeverStop.

I am grateful for these three things in my life

1. _____

2. _____

3. _____

I appreciate these two things about myself:

1. _____

2. _____

I am_____.

(POSITIVE AFFIRMATION)

There are times that the wrong relationships or situations will dissolve in life. Those things must leave our heart and mind in order for new and divine connections to be created and evolve.
Trust that better things are coming your way.

NeverStop.

I am grateful for these three things in my life

1. _____

2. _____

3. _____

I appreciate these two things about myself:

1. _____

2. _____

I am_____.
(POSITIVE AFFIRMATION)

If something makes you happy, it isn't a waste of time. The key is to know that happiness is a choice and a mental state, not something to be earned or purchased. Gratitude is the path to happiness. Love yourself and be patient with yourself. Don't look for sustained happiness in things that can be taken from you.

NeverStop.

I am grateful for these three things in my life

1. _____

2. _____

3. _____

I appreciate these two things about myself:

1. _____

2. _____

I am_____.
(POSITIVE AFFIRMATION)

There isn't always going to be a perfect time to do those things you are really wanting to do or are feeling pulled to do. Sometimes later becomes never. There is no better time than right now. We don't know how long we have so cherish every minute. Each moment is planned for us... to lift us up and to become prepared for the next moments.

NeverStop.

I am grateful for these three things in my life

1. _____

2. _____

3. _____

I appreciate these two things about myself:

1. _____

2. _____

I am_____.
(POSITIVE AFFIRMATION)

Try not to become overwhelmed with trying to do a lot more in every aspect of your life. Sometimes it just takes a little bit more. That little bit more effort, Focus, discipline, and Faith could make all of the difference. Focus each day on doing just a little bit more. Cherish each moment in life, it has divinely been planned for you.

NeverStop.

I am grateful for these three things in my life

1. _____

2. _____

3. _____

I appreciate these two things about myself:

1. _____

2. _____

I am_____.

(POSITIVE AFFIRMATION)

Always find and make time for the things that make you the happiest and calm your soul. It's easy to feel too busy but live life more out of intent, not just habit. It can be eye opening to evaluate "why" you do what you do. Start with gratitude and it will change the way you look at everything. Be present in the moment and don't get distracted by the next thing.

NeverStop.

I am grateful for these three things in my life

    1. _____

    2. _____

    3. _____

I appreciate these two things about myself:

    1. _____

    2. _____

I am_____.

(POSITIVE AFFIRMATION)

Always be true to yourself. Never lower your standards. No one can make us feel inferior without our permission. What we allow is what will continue. Always know your heart, mind, emotions, body, and desires matter. Know your worth. Have an open mind and a soft heart.

NeverStop.

I am grateful for these three things in my life

1. _____

2. _____

3. _____

I appreciate these two things about myself:

1. _____

2. _____

I am_____.
(POSITIVE AFFIRMATION)

Focus on finding a way to give back or to help someone on a daily basis. Not necessarily because they need help, but because you are a good person. Sometimes that's just what we need so that we can forget about ourselves for a moment. It allows us to see life from a different vantage point. Perform at least one good deed every day...it will inspire others to do the same.

NeverStop.

I am grateful for these three things in my life

1. _____

2. _____

3. _____

I appreciate these two things about myself:

1. _____

2. _____

I am_____.
(POSITIVE AFFIRMATION)

Love to live life one day at a time. Live with unwavering hope, faith, patience and optimism. Believe what is coming is better than what has gone. Enjoy the process of identifying your purpose. Sometimes we get to go through challenging times but believe it is only to prepare us for the great things coming our way.

NeverStop.

I am grateful for these three things in my life

1. _____

2. _____

3. _____

I appreciate these two things about myself:

1. _____

2. _____

I am_____.
(POSITIVE AFFIRMATION)

Appreciate the people around you...it makes a difference and it will encourage them to do more than what we expect. Appreciate not just what they do but who they are. Recognize people's value and show gratitude. Say thank you more than please. We have all been blessed with unique gifts.

NeverStop.

I am grateful for these three things in my life

1. _____

2. _____

3. _____

I appreciate these two things about myself:

1. _____

2. _____

I am_____.
(POSITIVE AFFIRMATION)

We learn by listening, not by talking. Listening is a way of showing that you are smart. Trust how you are smart, not just how smart you are. We are all a work in progress. Have a mind that is open to everything but attached to nothing. Embrace the pursuit of wisdom and understanding. Expand your mind, strengthen your body, and cultivate the Spirit within us.

NeverStop.

I am grateful for these three things in my life

1. _____

2. _____

3. _____

I appreciate these two things about myself:

1. _____

2. _____

I am_____.

(POSITIVE AFFIRMATION)

Sometimes we must sacrifice to improve our lives and create new habits. We must sacrifice anger in order to love. If not, you could sacrifice love because of anger. We must discipline ourselves and believe we can improve. Sacrifice our old ways to be made new. We have all of the strength we need.

NeverStop.

I am grateful for these three things in my life

1. _____

2. _____

3. _____

I appreciate these two things about myself:

1. _____

2. _____

I am_____.
(POSITIVE AFFIRMATION)

The secret to a fulfilling life is giving, not receiving. Give back without the intent of getting credit for it. Give with the spirit of gratitude, love and humbleness... not obligation or boastfulness. We have all been blessed with the opportunity to make a difference in someone's life.

NeverStop.

I am grateful for these three things in my life

1. _____

2. _____

3. _____

I appreciate these two things about myself:

1. _____

2. _____

I am_____.
(POSITIVE AFFIRMATION)

There is a big difference between simple and easy. Don't always look for easy. If we cut every corner, we end up just going in a circle. Put in the work, make a simple plan, and we will end up turning the corner and the trajectory of life with be in a new direction. Give all of the effort you can.

NeverStop.

I am grateful for these three things in my life

1. _____

2. _____

3. _____

I appreciate these two things about myself:

1. _____

2. _____

I am_____.

(POSITIVE AFFIRMATION)

We can't solve a problem with the same mind that created it. Invest in your mind and allow your mind to be made new. In order to have new thoughts, we have to let go of the old thoughts. Focus so much on progress that you don't even look for perfection.

NeverStop.

I am grateful for these three things in my life

1. _____

2. _____

3. _____

I appreciate these two things about myself:

1. _____

2. _____

I am_____.
(POSITIVE AFFIRMATION)

Let go of living to find security and start living for experiences. Collect knowledge and moments not things. Live life boldly and with optimism. Trust in the bigger plan when unique opportunities are brought into your life. Life is beautiful. Find joy in life.

NeverStop.

I am grateful for these three things in my life

1. _____

2. _____

3. _____

I appreciate these two things about myself:

1. _____

2. _____

I am_____.
(POSITIVE AFFIRMATION)

Learn good lessons from good friends. We can't give more than 100 %. If you're trying to give 110%, it just means that you haven't been giving 100 % all along. Do all that you can. Often times, effort means more than the outcome. Give 100% in all areas of your life. Be inspired by fulfilling your potential.

NeverStop.

I am grateful for these three things in my life

    1. _____

    2. _____

    3. _____

I appreciate these two things about myself:

    1. _____

    2. _____

I am_____.
(POSITIVE AFFIRMATION)

Happiness can be found in the way we live our life. Choose to live with love, grace, and gratitude. Once you fill your heart and mind with those kind of thoughts, peace and happiness will fill your soul. Be so full of these thoughts that you don't have room for anything negative. Smile often.

NeverStop.

I am grateful for these three things in my life

1. _____

2. _____

3. _____

I appreciate these two things about myself:

1. _____

2. _____

I am_____.
(POSITIVE AFFIRMATION)

Be in control of your emotions. Try not to let emotions control you. Anxiety... It often comes from worrying about things we cannot control. Do your best to not get worked up. Don't panic. Be disciplined and reflect on whether or not your anxiety is doing you any good. See your emotions as a strength not a weakness.

NeverStop.

I am grateful for these three things in my life

1. _____

2. _____

3. _____

I appreciate these two things about myself:

1. _____

2. _____

I am_____.
(POSITIVE AFFIRMATION)

Self-discipline begins with being in control of our thoughts. Once we have a clear direction with our thoughts, our actions will be aligned. For a real transformation of behavior, we must first change the way we think about things. Fill the mind with gratitude, love, patience, and optimism.

NeverStop.

I am grateful for these three things in my life

1. _____

2. _____

3. _____

I appreciate these two things about myself:

1. _____

2. _____

I am_____.
(POSITIVE AFFIRMATION)

It is better to be alone than in bad company. The key is to surround yourself with people that uplift you and force you to be your best. Uplift others and others will uplift you...you will attract those kinds of people. Not everyone is meant to stay in our lives forever but they were meant to be in our lives for a purpose.

NeverStop.

I am grateful for these three things in my life

1. _____

2. _____

3. _____

I appreciate these two things about myself:

1. _____

2. _____

I am_____.
(POSITIVE AFFIRMATION)

Visit TJSweet.net to learn more about how TJ can renew and improve mindsets

Facebook: TJ Sweet-The Gratitude Guy

Instagram: tjsweet__

Twitter: TJSweet__

LinkedIn: TJ Sweet

Podcast: Living the Sweet Life-TJ Sweet